CHRISTIAN REUNION
IN ECUMENICAL LIGHT

CHRISTIAN REUNION IN ECUMENICAL LIGHT

BY

FRANCIS J. HALL, D.D.

SOMETIME PROFESSOR OF DOGMATIC THEOLOGY IN
THE GENERAL THEOLOGICAL SEMINARY, NEW YORK;
MEMBER OF THE WORLD CONFERENCE COMMISSION OF
THE AMERICAN EPISCOPAL CHURCH; AND CO-OPTED
DELEGATE TO THE LAUSANNE CONFERENCE OF 1927

LONDON
SOCIETY FOR PROMOTING
CHRISTIAN KNOWLEDGE
NEW YORK AND TORONTO : THE MACMILLAN CO.
1930

Printed in Great Britain

FOREWORD

THOSE who are interested in the movement towards Christian Reunion, whatever their own views may be, will, I believe, welcome this book, written by one who holds high place in the world of theological scholarship, because it presents with complete candour, and also in the spirit of Christian love and sympathy, certain aspects of this great subject which must be kept in view if real progress is to be made.

The only adequate ideal and goal of Christian Reunion is the fulfilment of our Lord's own prayer ' that they all may be one.'

The author of this volume therefore emphasises the world-wide aspects of Reunion, and shows the impossibility of real advance without taking into full account the positions held by the Catholic world, which includes by far the greater part of Christendom. He urges that, while sympathising deeply with the movements to unite certain denominational Churches between which no important divergences of Faith and Order exist, the Anglican Churches, with the ultimate, world-wide vision before them, must stand faithful to those things which they hold in common with the whole of Catholic Christendom, the great essentials of Faith, Order, and Sacraments.

In the weighty words which he quotes, the endeavour of Anglicans must be ' not merely to meet difficulties and restore unity in our own country, but to do this in such a way as may form a basis for still wider union throughout the world. However remote the attainment of such an ideal may seem, we are responsible for seeing that nothing which we do now will create a new obstacle to that attainment.'

As baptised Christians, members of the one holy Catholic Church, our part in the work for Reunion, Catholics and Protestants alike, is not to create a new Church but the humbler one of ceasing to obstruct the unity and of helping to bring to its fuller realisation in this world the Church founded and commissioned by our Lord Jesus Christ Himself.

All will, I think, agree with the author that the cause of Reunion is not helped by ambiguous statements which ignore or conceal the differences among Christians, and many will welcome the presentation here given of the positions held by all Catholics, Anglican, Eastern, and Roman. The most encouraging fact in the situation to-day is the growing recognition that there are things sacred and essential which Catholicism has to give to Protestantism, and which Protestantism has to give to Catholicism.

The Lausanne Conference has shown us that it is possible for Christians to discuss their differences with the utmost frankness, not in the spirit of controversy, but with mutual sympathy and appreciation and with the desire to understand more fully the positions held by others.

The spirit which marked that Conference was felt by all in attendance to be a miracle of Divine grace and a true step on the way towards Reunion.

It is in that spirit that this book is written. I hope it may be read by many in the same spirit, and especially by those who are not in agreement with the author.

As he truly says, if we are to make progress towards a true and world-wide Reunion, both Protestants and Catholics must have ' sufficiently deep and patient love for each other frankly to face the differences which have been evaded, and seriously work for adequate mutual understanding concerning them.'

WILLIAM T. MANNING,
Bishop of New York.

PREFACE

My reason for adding another book to the growing literature concerning Christian Unity is the conspicuous lack in almost all of this literature of serious attention to the world-wide aspects of the subject. It does not seem to be realised that our Lord's prayer for the unity of His followers, and His relevant teaching, can be finally fulfilled and applied only by some visible form of corporate union of all Christendom in one world-wide fellowship.

I am in full sympathy with the steps being taken to unite certain denominational Churches between which no divergences of Faith and Order exist that are inconsistent with their union. But it is part of the argument of this book that those minor unions should not become reasons for evading the larger problem; and should not crystallise attitudes that will foreclose or hinder fresh, patient, and open-minded study of the questions of Faith and Order which have to be faced and agreed upon before full Christian union can become practical politics. The purpose for which the American Episcopal Church initiated the movement for a World Conference was just this, *to bring about co-operative and friendly study of these questions by all sections of Christendom.*

The aim of the present volume is to promote this purpose by emphasising the world-wide scope of the problem of unity, and by dealing with the questions of Faith and Order involved, as well as I can, ' in ecumenical light.' I mean in the light of principles which now control, and from the beginning have controlled, the outlook of the major part of Christendom.

During the past forty years I have given much study

to the problem of unity. I have read much of the relevant literature, both Catholic and Protestant, and have written many articles *ad rem* for different periodicals. I have also been a somewhat active member of the World Conference Commission of the American Episcopal Church since its first appointment in 1910, and took part as co-opted delegate in the Lausanne Conference in 1927. I have become more and more convinced that the only possible basis of full Christian Unity is that laid down by the American Bishops in 1886, ' the return of all Christian Communions to the principles of unity exemplified by the undivided Catholic Church during the first stages of its existence.' But I have come increasingly to realise how grave were the abuses and provocations which caused the Protestant revolt of the sixteenth century, how much sincere and zealous serving of Christ prevails among Protestants, and how necessary it is to do justice to certain principles emphasised by them. I was much edified by my contact with Protestant leaders at Lausanne.

I have striven earnestly to write this book without polemical animus. Its argumentative elements are designed simply to persuade those who are working in the interest of Christian unity, but have thus far omitted to reckon seriously with certain ancient principles, that these principles are worthy of patient consideration and will have to be faced and carefully studied before the problem of full Christian reunion can be successfully handled. Incidentally I have tried to interpret to Protestant readers certain baffling elements in the Anglican attitude toward current unity proposals.

My obligations, both to Catholic and to Protestant writers, are quite too numerous to specify here, and it has not seemed either necessary or desirable to complicate my book with footnotes and references. But I may not neglect to thank the Editors of *The Christian Union Quarterly; The Anglican Theological Review; The American Church Monthly;* and *The Living Church,* for permission to borrow from certain articles contributed by me to their pages. I must also express my grateful thanks to the good Bishop of New York, Dr. Manning, for his most kind Foreword.

I ought to explain that my purpose in confining the name Catholic to those Churches which retain the ancient threefold ministry, perpetuated by episcopal ordination, and the general sacramental and liturgical working system of the ancient undivided Church, and in designating other Churches as Protestant, is not contentious with reference either to the Catholic claim of certain Churches here called Protestant or to the fact that in certain regards the Anglican Church is Protestant. I am not calling Protestant Churches ' non-Catholic. I am simply following a widespread convention, being unable to find any other designations for the groups in question which are so generally intelligible. I hope my readers will acquit me of any polemical design.

CONTENTS

CHRISTIAN REUNION

CHAPTER I

AN ECUMENICAL PROBLEM

I. *Unity and Union*

WHAT do we mean by Christian Unity? The unreadiness of Christian leaders to devise satisfactory schemes for securing it is clear when we consider the confusing diversity of their answers to this question. Many are distinguishing sharply between unity and union and maintaining that union in any corporate sense is unnecessary for, even prejudicial to, unity.

Various substitutes for union are suggested, such as mutual recognition and comity between existing Churches, with more or less of occasional intercommunion and exchange of pulpits. There are also the Federations already adopted by certain Protestant Churches. They are intended to secure co-operation in matters of common interest, to enable the Churches to speak with united voice on moral questions of the day, and to reduce overlappings and rivalries in religious work, especially in the mission field. But they professedly leave the integrity of each Church, its confessional position, ministry, and general polity, untouched. Some supporters of Federation regard it as an emergency scheme only, hoping that it will prepare the way for corporate union. Others would go no further, believing that unity can be most satisfactorily actualised by the friendly relations and external co-operation which Federation is designed to secure.

On the other hand, an increasing number of Christians throughout the world are coming to see that the unity for which Christ prayed, and which alone can secure the *interior fellowship* upon which both the individual and social aspects of true religion depend for full actualisation, is necessarily corporate. They are agreed that without some effective form of general corporate union the full requirements of the Christian fellowship cannot be satisfied. This agreement is somewhat reduced in value, however, by the inability of many as yet to realise that the reunion of *all Christendom* is involved, and that the divisions to be removed include not only those existing within the Protestant and Catholic sections of Christendom, respectively considered, but also those between these sections at large. What is required is the reunion of all faithful Christians, whether Protestant or Catholic, in one world-wide organism.

Many are unready to believe such reunion to be possible. It is certainly not possible without the enlightening and assisting operation of the Holy Spirit. But this has been promised, and is plainly to be seen in the present stirring of Christian consciences on the subject of unity. Moreover, we may not think that the Lord prayed in vain when He prayed for a unity of His Church which should make it *visibly 'one flock.'* And we have to reckon with the rapid changes of civilisation and of general outlook now going on. In particular, no provincial outlook—not even the Roman—is escaping the influence of world-wide intercourse and interaction in things mental and spiritual as well as external. *Under divine overruling* the day will come, no doubt, when some world crisis will reveal the utter inadequacy of provincial and divisive traditions and standpoints. This will constrain men of good will to perceive things in juster proportions, and may with surprising quickness bring all real believers in Christ to a common mind touching the problem of reunion—a mind transcending the provincialisms of separated Churches and attaining the ecumenical.

All this may come very suddenly, but not less as the result of long preparation of men's minds by study and prayer, slowly producing by divine overruling a mentality which needs only some significant crisis to become conscious and articulate on truly ecumenical lines. Whether I am rightly picturing future developments or not, it should be perfectly plain to reflecting minds that only on the basis of an ecumenical outlook can the prayer of Christ be fulfilled that all may be one. The true preparation for such fulfilment is, therefore, the attainment by us all of the ecumenical standpoint. So long as our denominational affiliations and traditions prevent us from attaining this, so long will true and stable reunion of Christendom at large remain outside practical politics. And when these hindrances have been overcome, those who live in that glad day— perhaps long in coming—will be surprised at the pettiness and inconsequence of the saving of faces, the suspicious fears, and the ' flickering expedients,' which now blind our eyes and harden our hearts.

The aim of this book is to promote the growth—of myself as well as of others—towards the ecumenical mind. By the ecumenical mind I mean the mind imparted originally by Christ and His Holy Spirit to the Church, and which will be found paramount in that Church when its divisions are removed and all things provincial and adaptive are restored to their subordinate place and influence. To define and delimit precisely its content is as futile and unnecessary as to draw the line exactly between the light of an evening camp-fire and the surrounding darkness ; but I believe that the manner of its common attainment was rightly indicated by the American House of Bishops in 1886 when it affirmed that ' the Christian unity now so earnestly desired . . . can be restored only by the return of all Christian Communions to the principles of unity exemplified by the undivided Catholic Church during the first ages of its existence.'

II. *The Need of One Fellowship*

I need not elaborate the evils of Christian disunion : in particular, the overlappings and waste of Christian resources everywhere ; the consequent weakening and impoverishment of local organisations, engendering rivalries in the struggle for economic support and for the triumph of conflicting propagandas ; the inability of the Church to give united witness to the world in the moral questions continually arising, and effectively to proclaim the Christian message to heathen nations and to the unbelieving in Christian lands. I need not elaborate on them for this has been done by many competent writers.

But attention needs to be drawn more emphatically than is usually done to the impossibility of developing fully and widely the higher and more balanced aspects and elements of spiritual outlook and practice in mutually isolated and critically watchful organisations. No doubt each Church stands sponsor for and cultivates spiritual truths and practices of inestimable value ; but it does so with specialising onesidedness. Only a great world-wide Catholic Church, with free interplay of all temperaments and specialties of interest in one unobstructed fellowship, can prevent particular spiritual principles and interests from disproportionate emphasis and from running riot at the cost of caricature and of the spiritual impoverishment of multitudes.

The intrinsic nature and purpose of the fellowship which the Church was created by God to secure and safeguard also needs more careful attention in this connection. The fact that man is social by nature is coming to be recognised more adequately of late, as is also the corollary that the value of society to the individual depends upon its largeness, upon the reduction of provincial, national, and racial antagonisms, rivalries, and wars. Under purely secular conditions these limitations are chronic, and cannot wholly be removed. But even secular idealists increasingly perceive that it cannot be entirely well with mankind except upon the basis of some form of world-wide brotherhood, properly safeguarded from rupture. For example, wars cannot be effectively outlawed until their prevention is provided for by methods accepted as authoritative by mankind at large. Whether all my readers will agree with the precise form of my argument or not, I think they will acknowledge that the widening of peace, order, liberty, and progress depends upon the widening of social co-ordination along lines made effective by common consent.

This holds good in religion ; for man's nature requires that his life and progress should be socially conditioned in things pertaining to God and to his eternal future. Indeed, spiritual sociality is rooted in the triune Godhead. We are made in the image of God, and Christ expressly likens the unity of His disciples for which He prayed to that eternally subsisting between the divine Persons. The eternal life for which we are made is sharing in that divine social order—a chief mark of which is interior unity of the most absolute kind and result. The divine Three not only co-operate, but work *indivisibly* in all that they do. So it is that the Church is intended of God to be one both interiorly and visibly ; and division directly violates before the world the nature and function of the Church which God has established.

Our relations to God are social ; and our spiritual relations to each other are socially ordered by that fact as well as by our nature. The Christian covenant provides, therefore, that both our worship, whereby we express our relations to God, and God's bestowal of grace upon us shall be socially conditioned and effected in one body of Christ ; and that our private religious life and spiritual progress shall be linked up with this common social order. So it is that when the Church is divided, and Christians approach God in mutual isolation and in mutually discordant ways, the social aspect of true religion is reduced, the richness of spiritual life and character intended to be cultivated is impoverished, and love, the crowning glory thereof, is provincialised and diminished. In brief, the visible and corporate union of all Christendom is the central condition of adequate Christian developments on earth. *To promote the world-wide reunion of Christians, therefore, is of elementary requirement and urgency—not less so because the task involved is long, and apparently involves drastic changes in our denominational outlooks. Christ prayed for union, and ' God wills it.' It is a case of ' marching orders' from which no Christian appeal can rightly be attempted.*

The conviction that this is so explains why I am trying in this book to assume the ecumenical standpoint, that of the one great Church which Christ built, and which will again become manifest when its divisions are abolished and its wounds healed. From this standpoint, so far as I can attain it, that is, ' in ecumenical light,' I shall pursue the following order of treatment : The Anglican position and movement for reunion ; the proceedings and revelations of the Lausanne Conference ; the final or ecumenical conditions of reunion ; and various questions or issues involved.

The things that I believe are premature to discuss are the final ' terms ' or stipulations. I am convinced that when the Christian world is ready, and ecumenical union becomes practical politics, many of the so-called terms and reservations now ventilated or hinted at will cease to have their present bearing. The larger vision which will then emerge will surely precipitate a radical change in the estimate of the relative values of things. I do not mean that indifference to vital things will prevail. Far from it. But a juster estimate of what is vital and what is not will then be attained.

CHAPTER II

THE ANGLICAN POSITION

I TAKE up the subjects of this chapter and of the following one before proceeding further because of the prominent part which Anglican authorities have taken in recent unity discussions and because, as I think will appear, I shall thus most successfully prepare the way for my main purpose of considering the whole problem of ' Christian Reunion in Ecumenical Light.'

I. *Why Frequently Misunderstood*

Owing to its wide tolerance of mutually conflicting schools of thought and practice, and to the adoption by many of its leaders of the policy of comprehension—of seeking to secure legitimate room therein for Conservatives and Modernists and for Anglo-Catholics and Evangelical Protestants—the position of the Anglican Communion is diversely interpreted by its own leaders and is not easily understood by non-Anglicans.

This difficulty is increased, even for the intelligent, by the fact that the writings and utterances which are most apt to be ventilated in the press, in theological literature of the moment, and especially in current reviews and newspapers, are not adequately representative. They are of the startling and innovating kind, striking contributions to current questions, and such novel pronouncements as provide ' news.' To the outer world the utterances and books which are most representative, most in accord with established and permanent Anglican thought, are not sufficiently challenging to demand attention. To the majority they have the lack of interest of an old story that has grown stale.

Non-Anglican Protestants and Catholics alike are also apt to look primarily to unofficial Anglican literature, rather than to our official formularies and prescriptions, in investigating the Anglican position. Protestants do so because of their habitually low estimate of the significance of authoritative ecclesiastical requirements, and Catholics because of their tendency to regard the extreme tolerance shown by Anglican authorities as evidence that these requirements are negligible.

This conclusion, however, disagrees with the situation and with the historical explanation of Anglican tolerance. Three significant facts are overlooked. The *first* is that all three of the schools—Catholic, Evangelical, and Liberal—which have developed within the Anglican Communion have all along accepted one Book of Common Prayer as authoritative ; and, in the main, have conformed to its general requirements as they have honestly understood them. Very few indeed either profess or think that rejection of the authority of that book is consistent with Anglicanism. Needless to say, the Prayer Book embodies a recognisable working system both of Faith and of Order.

The *second* fact is that toleration of whatever degree, so long as thus regarded, implies a recognised authoritative norm, coupled in this case with belief that, except in very extreme emergencies, patience is more likely in the long run to secure loyalty to the Church's teaching and practice than formal discipline. Such has notoriously been the ordinary excuse of Anglican authorities for pursuing the policy of toleration. And it is frequently based avowedly upon the Lord's instruction that we should not root up the tares lest in so doing we also root up the wheat.

The *third* fact, accounting for the origin and unique

degree of Anglican toleration, without at all nullifying the determinate significance of the Prayer Book system that received authoritative enactment, is the policy adopted by the Crown and observed under its influence by the English Church during the Reformation period, the policy of striving by every defensible means to retain the allegiance to the national Church of all the nation. The determination that no new religion should be established preserved Anglican continuity with the past; but *Articles of Religion* were framed which were designedly vague in many particulars, with the intention of affording a platform to which all the existing factions could agree without rejecting undeniable articles of the Catholic Faith and without formal heresy. This policy was eirenic in intention, but failed to be so in effect because of the coercive methods with which its fulfilment was undertaken. But when the principle of toleration gained its modern acceptance, the original desire to unite all Englishmen in one national Church accentuated that principle, and made the future exercise of ecclesiastical discipline obnoxious. Moreover, the spirit of toleration thus accentuated has naturally spread through the Anglican Communion at large, even in the parts of it which are most free from the conditions of the 'establishment.'

II. *Its Real Nature*

The general result, on the one hand, is that the Anglican Communion expressly conforms to, and prescribes, the traditional Catholic system in its fundamental elements of faith, ministry, sacraments, worship, and discipline, thereby continuing to rank itself with Catholic rather than with Protestant Churches.[1] On the other hand, this Communion, along with Protestants, has rejected papal jurisdiction, and has purged out certain non-primitive accretions to the Catholic system. And in

[1] See the Preface for explanation of the use of the terms 'Catholic' and 'Protestant' in this volume.

the interest of retaining those who would go further and break away from the Catholic system, it has put a soft note into some of its teaching and has made possible the development of a unique degree of freedom of opinion in its midst.

I think the above represents a substantially correct understanding of the Anglican standpoint; but I have available the very weighty exposition of it, entitled 'Anglicanism,' by Dr. W. H. Carnegie, Sub-Dean of Westminster.[1] It should be studied by all who would understand the deeper factors that make Anglicanism what it is—fundamentally the same since the English Church was organised in the seventh century.

Dr. Carnegie shows convincingly that 'Institutional continuity on its outer side, intense traditionalism on its inner—these are the master features of English life in all its chief aspects and activities.' 'The Anglican Church has maintained its institutional continuity by virtue of its strong traditionalism, by virtue of the instinctive reverence with which its members have all along been disposed to regard the teachings of past experience.' This, it seems to me, explains Anglican opportunism, the readiness to be influenced by new movements without pursuing them radically to their logical end. Each succeeding convulsion has left Anglicanism 'modified, it may be in form, and enriched in content, but unaltered in essential character and direction.' The papal factor, the Calvinistic influence, Latitudinarianism and Sentimentalism, Romanticism, Scientific Materialism, Biblical Criticism, Agnosticism, and Industrialism, as Dr. Carnegie shows, have severally illustrated this.

Romanticism or Tractarianism, unlike the other influences mentioned, as Dr. Carnegie says, 'revived the historical consciousness of the Anglican Church, and that consciousness once roused became a dominating factor in her activities.' 'Tractarianism restored Anglican Traditionalism to clear self-consciousness and

[1] London and New York, 1925.

provided it with effective means of luminous self-expression. Hence came its widespread influence. This has extended far beyond the circle of its declared adherents, and has become a factor which has to be taken into serious account in any estimate of contemporary Church life.' I add, also, in estimating what Anglicans in general will ultimately think and do in relation to reunion. Dr. Carnegie proceeds to say ' that the great majority of instructed and intelligent Churchmen of the present day, whatever their professed affinities or antagonisms, start from Tractarian assumptions, and accept Tractarian ideals, and approach the consideration of the religious problem from the Tractarian standpoint.'

' In practice, if not in theory,' he says, ' the great majority of earnest Churchmen nowadays are Sacramentalists, and their sacramentalism is one of the signs and outcomes of their *traditional* consciousness, reawakened by Tractarianism.' ' The prevalent conception of the Christian life is that of a continuous growth, mediated and maintained by interconnected sacramental ordinances. Low Churchmen may differ from High Churchmen, Evangelicals from Catholics, in their doctrinal expositions of the manner in which the Holy Spirit acts through these. But the ordinances themselves they set great store by, and use them as the main medium and implement of their pastoral activities.'

So far Dr. Carnegie proceeds, with argument not safely to be disregarded by Nonconformists in estimating the present trend of thought and practice among Anglicans. And this trend is no interruptive and non-significant phenomenon, but is a quickening of the deepest and most abiding undercurrent of Anglican developments from the beginning.

It is not difficult to show that Anglican sacramentalism reflects faithfully the official and constitutional position of the Anglican Churches. And this affords evidence that the tradition which has kept Anglicans faithful to the past—a past reaching far beyond the Reformation—

is the Catholic tradition. The Reformation resulted in putting a soft pedal upon certain Catholic notes among Anglicans. But no real breach of continuity occurred, whether hierarchical, liturgical, or sacramental. Accordingly, when reactionary sentiments had grown less violent, and Anglicans began slowly to find themselves again, it was the ancient Catholic working system, retained in fundamentals in the Prayer Book, that mainly determined subsequent developments. Each revival of devotion to the prescribed ways of the Prayer Book has resulted in a Catholic movement. And each movement of this kind, Laudian, Restorationist, and Tractarian, has brought into clearer light the outstanding fact that officially, and in its prescribed working system, the English Church and her daughter Churches belong to the Catholic group of Churches. And the liberties which Anglicans in general cherish are Catholic liberties.

III. *Anglo-Catholic Factor*

The Anglo-Catholic movement is a continuation of the Tractarian movement. Although more advanced in surface particulars, and attended in some quarters by incidental developments not widely approved, its fundamental sacramentalism is being increasingly emphasised, even among those who refuse any affiliation with the Anglo-Catholic *party*. And this is due to the fact that the Prayer Book is clearly patient of sacramentalist interpretation, indeed to an important degree requires it. In brief, Anglo-Catholicism, in its fundamentals at least, is at home in the Anglican Churches. It does not have to be tolerated, since it represents a recovery of the most abiding and most determinative Anglican tradition. As the ' spear-head ' of Anglican traditionalism, the Anglo-Catholic *party* is distinctly in the minority ; but it is the ' spear-head ' of a movement by which a large majority of Anglicans are either consciously or unconsciously influenced. Moreover, this vaster movement does not appear to be conditioned for its vital continuance upon the fortunes of the party in question.

I am taking a large part of my space to exhibit the Catholic nature of the Anglican position because its non-realisation by Nonconformists has hindered them from perceiving the representative aspect of Anglo-Catholic resistance to schemes for mutual ministerial recognition, occasional communion, and so forth. This resistance, although most vocal among Anglo-Catholics, is approved by an effective proportion of Anglicans.

Reminding my readers of the world-wide, ecumenical aim of the Anglican movement for reunion, I venture to maintain that, *if Nonconformists seriously seek to unite with Anglicans in this movement, they have need carefully to reckon with, and therefore adequately to understand, the Anglo-Catholic position.* It has representative value to a peculiarly significant degree ; and its importance for the problem of reunion does not at all lie in the number of those who adhere to the Anglo-Catholic *party*, or approve of all its incidental developments.

(*a*) In fundamental substance its leading contentions simply freshen and bring into sharp relief the sacramentalism which, as Dr. Carnegie shows, is traditionally implicit in Anglicanism.

(*b*) This sacramentalism, although often softened in expression, is retained in its most vital particulars in the Prayer Book. It is therefore an integral element of the official mind of the Anglican Communion.

(*c*) Although Rome denies the place of Anglo-Catholics in the Church, and the Orthodox Easterns are not fully satisfied that they truly represent Anglicanism, their several positive principles plainly are, and from ancient times have been, maintained by seven-tenths of Christendom, as being integral parts of Christianity from the beginning.

In the light of this, it is not difficult to perceive why every scheme for action looking to reunion between

Nonconformists and Anglicans, even when advocated by prominent Anglican leaders, is defeated by Anglican inertia. The reason is that the majority of thoughtful Anglicans believe these schemes to be premature until certain vital questions are settled which have not as yet been seriously faced. And they cannot be faced adequately so long as Anglo-Catholicism itself is dismissed from examination as being an anomalous and non-representative factor in the situation.

These considerations should not be taken as justifying abandonment of the present movement for reunion. God forbid! They simply bring into clear relief the contention that the work before us all, in particular between Nonconformists and Anglicans, is educational. And our conferences should not be embarrassed by forcing the pace with premature proposals.

The Catholic aspects of Anglicanism, though unequally realised by Anglicans, represent the hold that the ecumenical standpoint still retains upon them ; and, as is maintained in this volume, true Christian Union can be understood only ' in ecumenical light.'

CHAPTER III

THE ANGLICAN MOVEMENT FOR REUNION

THE Anglican movement for reunion—initiated at Chicago in 1886, given educational method at Cincinnati in 1910, and revealing both its largeness of outlook and its dangers at Lambeth in 1920—has helped to develop world-wide realisation of the evils flowing from Christian divisions, and general interest in the problem of reunion. On the other hand, as the movement has advanced the dangers by which its promotion is inevitably beset are clearly emerging.

I am not a pessimist. I confidently believe that, whatever may be the outcome of the movement in the near future, in particular of the World Conference movement, much is being achieved that is worth while. The Holy Spirit is working ; and even if reactions occur and present hopes are deferred, some day the movement will be resumed with better prospects. Future workers will have gained wisdom from considering present failures. The causes that now hinder mutually separated Christians from adequately and patiently grappling with difficulties will then be more generally realised, and later promoters of unity will profit by present mistakes.

None the less, it is our duty to make the most of the present movement, and as part of this duty to realise and shun the dangers which, if not avoided, will seriously reduce the progress which can be made in this generation. I say, ' in this generation,' for under the most favourable conditions the task of world-wide Christian reunion is quite too large for one generation to complete.

I believe that it is worth while at this point to give a review of the Anglican movement for reunion, with a view to emphasising the corporate principles which have determined its method, even as against misleading utterances and schemes of some of its leading promoters. If in doing this I seem to be unduly critical, the reason is that the success of the movement depends upon realising and combating the dangers that attend it.

I. *Anglican Leadership*

The present movement for Christian reunion is undoubtedly due to the Holy Spirit; but, humanly speaking, it was given its initial and definitive direction in 1886, by the Declaration on Unity of our American House of Bishops. And, although the movement has since enlisted the co-operation of leaders in many Christian bodies, both Catholic and Protestant, Anglicans continue to be especially conspicuous in its promotion. The reason seems clear, viz. that the Anglican Communion has vital points of contact with every section of Christendom.

In common with the Roman Catholic and Orthodox Eastern Churches, this Communion retains, in spite of non-essential variations, the ancient Catholic Faith and Order—the Catholic Creeds, and doctrinal decrees of the ancient Ecumenical Councils; the historic ministry of bishops, priests, and deacons, uninterruptedly transmitted from primitive times; the sacraments, administered essentially after the primitive manner; and the Catholic working system of liturgical Eucharistic worship, of the ecclesiastical calendar, and of the main lines of spiritual discipline. Even under the confusing conditions of the sixteenth century, the appeal to antiquity served to keep the Anglican Church in line with its Catholic past. We are also agreed, on the one hand, with the Roman Church, in retaining various Western forms of theological thought, and, on the other hand, with the Eastern Churches in rejecting the Vatican claims.

In rejecting these claims we go a certain distance at least with Protestants, and in this limited respect the American Episcopal Church describes itself as ' Protestant.' Moreover, while we consider that Nonconforming Protestants have abandoned vital parts of the ancient Christian system, we accept the main positive elements of their Evangelical Faith as fundamental to the Christian position. Still further, while we cannot regard their rejection of the Catholic ministry and working system as in harmony with the will of Christ for His Church, we acknowledge the sincerity of their devotion to Christ, and are confirmed thereby in the conviction that the visible fruits of their devotion are evidences of the Holy Spirit's blessing.

These points of sympathy might be elaborated, but it should be sufficient for my argument to refer to the patent fact that the Anglican Communion has retained and cherished groups of churchmen of diverse types controlled by the tendency to emphasise respectively the distinctive principles of one or other of the several non-Anglican divisions of Christendom. No Catholic and no Protestant position, positively considered, fails to gain sympathetic approval among Anglicans. Is it strange that, under such circumstances, many should regard the Anglican Communion as peculiarly equipped to be ' the Church of the Reconciliation ' ?

II. *The Initial Declaration of* 1886

' The Quadrilateral,' as it is called, appeared originally in 1886, as part of the American bishops' Declaration on Unity, above mentioned.[1] It has been widely misunderstood, because considered in isolation from its

[1] *Journal of the General Convention of* 1886, p. 80.

context, and treated as a formal and therefore complete list of conditions of reunion. In fact, the whole Declaration in question is didactic, and expressly leaves the question of definitive ' conditions ' of reunion to future conference and study. Inasmuch as this Declaration defines more clearly than any other official document the fundamental standpoint and guiding principles which necessarily determine the general method and the practical possibilities of corporate Anglican action with regard to reunion, it ought to be studied most carefully.

After several eirenic preliminaries, including acknowledgment that all duly baptised Christians are members of the Catholic Church, and a disclaimer of desire to absorb other Christian Communions into the Episcopal Church, the bishops define the fundamental prerequisite of Christian reunion in the following terms :

' We do hereby affirm that the Christian unity now so earnestly desired . . . can be restored only by the return of all Christian Communions to the principles of unity exemplified by the undivided Catholic Church during the first ages of its existence ; which principles we believe to be the substantial deposit of Christian Faith and Order committed by Christ and His Apostles to the Church unto the end of the world, and therefore incapable of compromise or surrender by those who have been ordained to be its stewards and trustees for the common and equal benefit of all men.'

In this Declaration four points should be noted : (*a*) the bishops adhere faithfully to the principle of appeal to antiquity that determined the direction and limits of the Anglican Reformation ; (*b*) the Church, the unity of which is in view, is not one that is to be built hereafter by aggregation of diverse denominations of Christians, but is the original and still existing Catholic Church ; (*c*) the world-wide aspect of the problem is put to the fore, ' all Christian Communions,' ' for the common and equal benefit of all men ' ; (*d*) the essential conditions of reunion, whatever incidental stipulations may have to be made in order to secure mutual understanding and working harmony within the reunited Church, are confined to 'the substantial deposit of Christian Faith and Order committed by Christ and His Apostles to the Church unto the end of the world.'

The bishops proceed to give, not a comprehensive list of these essentials, but certain leading particulars which should be reckoned with at the outset in discussions of the conditions of unity. The bishops appear rightly to assume that real agreement concerning these particulars will effectively clear the way to more comprehensive accord. So they proceed to declare—

'As inherent parts of this sacred deposit, and therefore as essential to the restoration of unity among the divided branches of Christendom, we account the following, to wit:

'1. The Holy Scriptures of the Old and New Testament as the revealed Word of God.

'2. The Nicene Creed as the sufficient statement of the Christian Faith.

'3. The two Sacraments—Baptism and the Supper of the Lord—ministered with unfailing use of Christ's words of institution and of the elements ordained by Him.

'4. The Historic Episcopate, locally adapted in the methods of its administration to the varying needs of the nations and peoples called of God into the unity of His Church.'

It is to be noted: (*a*) that although the Nicene Creed does not specify all necessary Christian doctrines, it is sufficient for Creed purposes, and, when sincerely accepted, leads the believer on to a full Christian faith; (*b*) that the requirements as to the so-called minor sacraments, and as to a liturgical form of Eucharistic worship, are in no wise abandoned. They remain for future conferences to consider; (*c*) the Historic Episcopate is given explicitly as one of the 'inherent parts of this sacred deposit,' the deposit from Christ and His Apostles. The common impression that it is specified only as in widespread and long-established possession, and simply on this ground practically necessary to be retained in a reunited Christendom, is demonstrably out of accord with explicit contents of the Declaration.

The bishops conclude with expression of ' our desire and readiness . . . to enter into brotherly conference with all or any Christian bodies . . . with a view to the *earnest study* of the conditions under which so priceless a blessing might be brought to pass ' (italics mine).

The Lambeth Conference of 1888 adopted and published the four particulars, or ' Quadrilateral ' as it had come to be called (unfortunately in isolation from the main Declaration that makes clear its background), as basis of discussion of ' home reunion '—reunion with British Nonconformists. This no doubt helped to establish the above-mentioned misinterpretation of the Declaration—as meaning that acceptance of the Quadrilateral, regardless of its background and of other conditions, would be treated by the Anglican Communion as sufficient for reunion.

Two solid reasons forbid such a conclusion. In the *first* place, the Declaration of 1886 still stands as the most definite official statement of the Anglican position with regard to reunion. The failure of the Lambeth Conference to take over the whole of it did not signify any departure from it, but was due to special and opportunist aims of the moment. Moreover, the pronouncement of the Lambeth Conference of 1920, subject to criticism in some details though it be, obviously preserves the world-wide outlook and Catholic background of the American Declaration.

Secondly, the striking enlargement and increased influence of the Anglo-Catholic movement has given renewed emphasis to the historic appeal of the Anglican Communion to antiquity, and has immensely fortified the ecumenical Catholic outlook of Anglicans. No plan of reunion which fails to make the ancient Catholic system paramount can be adopted to-day by Anglican authorities without hopelessly dividing Anglicans among themselves.

These are facts to be reckoned with, whatever may be our sentiments with regard to them; and failure to reckon with them will bring disillusionment and a real setback to the cause of Christian reunion.

III. *The World Conference Movement*

The World Conference proposal was a logical sequel of the American bishops' Declaration of 1886. In that declaration they had striven to transcend provincialism, and to keep in view the world-wide aspects of Christian unity. It was from an explicitly ecumenical standpoint that they invited conference for free discussion of the conditions of unity. The only official response came from the Presbyterians in 1887; and they withdrew from conference in 1896, because they could not secure official acceptance from us of the stipulation that 'mutual recognition and reciprocity' of ministries should be presupposed in the conference.

The propositions of our so-called 'Quadrilateral' were didactic. They indicated certain positions maintained by this Church as being obvious subject-matters of conference. They were not given as premises of conference required to be accepted by all participants at the outset. The bishops aimed to secure conference on *all* obstacles to Christian unity, and such conference could not be had if determinations of questions at issue were to be required in advance. But, as I have already indicated, the exclusiveness of attention paid to the 'Quadrilateral,' isolated from the rest of the Declaration, prevented a just understanding; and the World Conference plan, adopted in 1910 by the General Convention at Cincinnati, was designed to make more clear, and to bring to effective realisation, the original conference proposal of 1886. It is only by attention to this logical connection, and to the whole Declaration of 1886 above given, that the World Conference proposal can be rightly understood, and certain misapprehensions can be removed—misapprehensions in which many of our own people share.

(*a*) No presuppositions were required for taking part in the Conference except the most central and essential article of Christian faith, that Jesus Christ is ' God and Saviour.' This did not mean that the several Christian bodies which participated threw their treasured principles into solution, and committed themselves to treating them as subject-matters of compromise or of adjudication by the Conference. It simply meant that every difference of Faith and Order that now divides the Christian world should be faced frankly and courteously, and freely discussed. The aim was educational, to promote that mutual understanding which is the indispensable condition of ' the return of all Christian Communions to the principles of unity exemplified by the undivided Catholic Church during the first ages of its existence . . . the substantial deposit of Christian Faith and Order committed by Christ and His Apostles to the Church unto the end of the world.'

(*b*) In order that no fear of entanglement in compromising actions or pronouncements should prevent any Christian body from participating, the purpose of the proposed Conference was explicitly limited to ' study and discussion without power to legislate or to adopt resolutions.' And it was not proposed as a Conference on Unity ; and was not to be concerned with schemes to bring it about. The proposal was based upon the conviction that an unembarrassed discussion of questions of Faith and Order for mutual understanding ' is the next step toward unity,' and should be the sole business of the Conference. Sacerdotalists and anti-sacerdotalists, therefore, Catholics and Protestants, could freely take part without in the slightest degree prejudicing or imperilling their several convictions. Even if in the outcome the Conference had exceeded its prescribed limitations, and had been swept emotionally into doubtful resolutions or pronouncements, these results, while they would have reduced, perhaps have ruined, the value of the Conference, could not have committed any participating Communion. They would have had no authority whatever.

(c) This Church led the way in inviting other Communions, but carefully refrained from assuming any dominance in the Conference. All were to ' come in on the ground floor.' They were ' asked to unite with us in arranging for and conducting ' the Conference. Accordingly, our Joint Commission appointed for the purpose confined itself to the business of engaging participation, and over eighty bodies united in the plan, the Roman Catholic Church being the only considerable Communion that did not officially accept our invitation. Much non-official interest, however, was shown by its writers. The business of ' arranging for and conducting ' the Conference came under the control of a Continuation Committee, appointed in 1920, and containing representatives of the principal bodies participating in the plan.

Some of our people feared that the Continuation Committee would not be sufficiently mindful of the limitation originally stipulated for the proposed Conference ; and that the programme would be so arranged as to side-track thorny questions which ought to be freely discussed.

Some perception of this, and considerable fears of entanglement in premature and misleading commitments, largely explain the difficulty experienced in securing active interest in the World Conference movement among Anglo-Catholics. Some of them indeed took part ; but generally speaking, these churchmen held aloof. They were more alive to the dangers I am defining than to the limited and justifiable purpose of the Conference. And they failed to see that if the Conference should succumb to its dangers it would in any case leave the Catholic Church uncommitted. Probably its very failure would teach those concerned how large and prolonged must be the task of bringing Catholics and Protestants to that measure of agreement in questions of Faith and Order which is the essential condition of wholesome and abiding reunion.

At this point a few remarks may be ventured on certain *ad interim* statements, signed jointly by Anglican and Nonconformist leaders, that have been issued from time to time during the past decade, partly in direct connection with the World Conference movement, and partly as a result of conferences held under the auspices of the Archbishop of Canterbury since the last Lambeth Conference. Their common purpose has been to define agreements concerning Faith and Order, and concerning some of the conditions of reunion—definitions of limited range, but designed to clear the ground for progress in discussing other questions and conditions. An examination of these statements proves that in the main they have been carefully and skilfully composed, and have been signed not only in an eirenic spirit, but with grave sense of responsibility. The lofty tone and purpose, the competence and standing of those who have signed them, and the fact that they ostensibly define agreements between Anglicans and Nonconformists not previously acknowledged, these circumstances established their importance and demand their respectful and patient consideration.

But the point of view from which they ought to be examined and estimated is their value for enlarging mutual understanding between Anglicans and Nonconformists *in general*, and their effect in promoting or retarding the larger aim of *world-wide* Christian reunion. When thus examined, the statements in question reveal not only important limitations but serious drawbacks. I cannot take space to discuss them in detail, but confine myself to certain broad defects which the several discussions that have followed their publication appear to have established, common to them all, although in varying degrees.

(*a*) They all contain more or less ambiguous language, ambiguous in vital aspects of the questions sought to be answered. And subsequent discussions reveal the fact that they have been signed in mutually discordant meanings. In other words, certain leading propositions are not as significant as they have been thought to be. The agreements which they express, although important, are not very comprehensive. Significant disagreements are side-tracked, and the statements in question are to a degree merely illusory verbal platforms. Their effect is to postpone questions which, so long as they are evaded, will reduce the value of conference in other matters. The Catholic doctrine of the ministry, for example, cannot be enveloped in eirenic phrases of ambiguous meaning with reasonable hope of progress in mutual understanding between Anglicans and Nonconformists. Still more obviously it cannot as between Catholic and Protestant bodies in general.

(*b*) In so far as these statements express real agreement between those who have signed them, they register progress in mutual understanding for which we ought to be thankful, provided the agreements are such as can finally be approved sincerely both by Nonconformists at large and by the Anglican and other Catholic Churches. But, and this is an important limitation, the progress thus really achieved is that of only a few scholars in conference. It is one with which the vast majority of their co-religionists have not caught up. And this fact holds whether we reckon with the subject-matters of agreement or with the decidedly exceptional temper and atmosphere of these conferences. My point is that there is danger of exaggerating the progress which these statements appear to register, and that such exaggeration is likely to result finally in disillusionment and discouragement. The statements, at their best, are *ad interim* only. They must be followed by much conference and much education ; and they have not assumed, cannot yet assume, a form that can satisfy all who have to be satisfied before actual steps toward reunion can be safely undertaken.

In general, the habit of publishing statements of agreement exclusively is open to two serious objections. In the first place, as has already been indicated, such statements give an illusory impression. They lead men to think that a stage has been reached at which acceptable schemes of reunion, as between Anglicans and Nonconformists at least, can be devised. The fact is that the most serious obstacles to such reunion are not seriously faced. And this suggests the second objection, that a habit is being hardened of evading these more serious obstacles. The important group of questions associated with what is called ' sacerdotalism ' and ' sacramentalism ' have to be directly reckoned with. So long as the sacerdotal and anti-sacerdotal sections of Christendom lack sufficient mutual love to confer frankly, and at the same time kindly and patiently, with each other concerning these questions, they are not ready to take practical steps of any kind toward reunion.

In support of what I am urging I venture to quote a weighty passage in the late Bishop (Burge) of Oxford's *Contemporary Review* article on ' Reunion.' He writes that ' no visible unity is worth having, indeed it would be shattered in a generation, if it is produced by diplomatic language, and is the result of political arrangement. All parties must mean the same thing and know that they mean the same thing.'

It was on this rock of opposed interpretations that the attempted Concordat between the Congregational and Episcopal Churches in America went to pieces. The Congregationalists sought for Episcopal ordination simply as a means of developing a ministry that would be more generally recognised as valid. A large and responsible section of Episcopalians, on the other hand, regarded it as formal sanction of the policy of conferring priesthood on those who notoriously did not believe in priesthood and who would continue to use their ministry on a non-sacerdotal basis. The doctrine of priesthood was involved, and the evident opposition of convictions concerning this doctrine converted a well-meant step towards future reunion into a new cause of friction and disillusionment. The whole action led into a blind alley.

Unless both Protestants and Catholics have sufficiently deep and patient love for each other frankly to face the differences which have been evaded, and seriously work for adequate mutual understanding concerning them, their efforts to promote a true and world-wide reunion will fail. The time has not come for schemes. A campaign of education—probably a prolonged one—is the only feasible ' next step toward unity.' It is to such a campaign that the Holy Spirit is calling us at present. We need many conferences, unembarrassed by pressure for immediate visible results.

IV. *The Lambeth Conference of* 1920

The Lambeth Conference of 1920 adopted a series of resolutions on unity and issued ' An Appeal to all Christian People.' Its language has encouraged many to hope that effective practical steps toward reunion, in particular between Anglicans and Nonconformists, may be taken in this generation. Such hopes, however, I believe to be premature. They are not warranted by any real prospect of sufficient removal in the near future of the disagreements which, while they continue, preclude wholesome and permanent reunion. They are largely based upon diplomacy, made impressive by its truly Christian and loving spirit, and upon the illusion that a loving will to unite can do duty for a common mind in the determinative elements of Christian Faith, Order, discipline, and worship.

The Lambeth pronouncement is in certain respects most notable. Its spirit is splendid, so splendid indeed that, open to criticism as some of its propositions are, its defects are not likely to nullify its influence in deepening

the mutual good will that is the first condition of progress
in conference toward mutual understanding and toward
the common Catholic mind upon which healthful reunion
depends. None the less, while its standpoint is clearly
ecumenical and Catholic, so that it has been received with
a degree of approval by some Anglo-Catholic churchmen,
the optimism of its framers as to possibilities of progress
toward reunion in the near future has led to the inclusion
of premature proposals, and to language that is illusory
and unsatisfactory because ambiguous. Several illustra-
tions may be given.

(*a*) The bishops say, ' We believe that for all, the truly
equitable approach to Union is by way of mutual deference to one another's consciences.' This language is
ambiguous. Very likely the bulk of the bishops meant
merely to define the spirit in which present conferences
should be conducted—that we should not be impatient
with those who are as yet unable conscientiously to agree
with us. But this is not clear. The language used is
readily taken to mean that divergence of conscience concerning the things that now divide Christendom need
not prevent reunion, if we agree mutually to disregard
or tolerate them. In brief, a shelving, rather than a
removal, of them seems to many to be suggested. Only
if we qualify the bishops' language by making it refer
exclusively to non-essentials, can we justify such a proposal. In the field of convictions that determine consciences as to corporate Faith, Order, and common
worship a common mind is indispensable. ' Mutual
deference to one another's consciences ' when reunion
takes place must have become unnecessary in determinative matters as between the Christian Communions that
reunite. It is to be remembered that the ' Appeal ' is
concerned with conditions of corporate reunion—not
with the tolerance that may be practised toward the weak
consciences of particular private individuals. It is agreement in the determinative elements of Faith and Order
—not mutual deference in conscientious disagreement—

that is required for reunion. The point is vital. We must frankly face our disagreements, and the general failure thus far to do this is proof that the mutual understandings and agreements which will make schematic proposals worth while are not yet in sight.

(*b*) The bishops ' would say that if the authorities of other Communions should so desire, we are persuaded that, *terms of union having been otherwise satisfactorily adjusted* ' (italics mine), ' Bishops and Clergy of our Communion would willingly accept from these authorities a form of commission or recognition which would commend our ministry to their congregations, as having its place in one common life. . . . It is our hope that the same motive would lead ministers who have not received it to accept a commission through episcopal ordination, as obtaining for them a ministry throughout the whole fellowship. In so acting no one of us could possibly be taken to repudiate his past ministry. God forbid that any man should repudiate a past experience rich in spiritual blessings for himself and others. . . .'

This language, as Nonconformists have quickly perceived, contains an important ambiguity. The bishops suggest mutual interchange of ministerial commission or recognition, but describe the proposed commission of Nonconformists by us as ' episcopal ordination.' Nonconformists naturally ask if this does not imply the invalidity of their previous ordination. The unexpressed fact that we cannot consistently acknowledge the validity of such ordinations for the Catholic Church no doubt explains the bishops' halting language ; but the result is not happy.

In any case, their proposal is hopelessly premature. That the suggested double procedure will be either necessary or desirable when terms of union have been ' otherwise satisfactorily adjusted ' is very doubtful indeed. When that glad day arrives the anxiety for ' saving of faces ' will undoubtedly be completely overshadowed on all sides by the joy of union under one

Faith and Order. And so long as Nonconformists require explicit recognition of the spiritual claims of their denominational ministries, they will be handicapped in facing the real question—'What common ministry answers to the will of Christ for His universal Church?' Very few churchmen fail to perceive that the Holy Spirit has blessed the work of non-episcopal ministers. But to require or concede an acknowledgment of this in formal action or concordat is to include among the terms of reunion what is not essential to the reunited Church. It is likely also to imply a view which Catholic Churches cannot consistently affirm—the view that the origination of non-episcopal ministries was consistent with the arrangements of Christ for His Church.

(c) Closely related to the above are the proposals, under the same conditions—that is, when actual reunion is being satisfactorily advanced—to permit the interchange of pulpits and the occasional admission of Nonconformists to the privilege of communicating at our altars.

These proposals are also premature. The conditions under which they are suggested do not exist, and do not appear to be yet in sight. Therefore the effect of such proposals is to encourage uncanonical irregularities ; and an unsettlement of the internal discipline and order of the Anglican Communion is not favourable to the cause of unity. It upsets the peace of loyal churchmen, creates internal disunity, and brings the whole reunion movement under suspicion. The bishops at Lambeth failed to realise that many of those who were to read their optimistic suggestions did not at all understand the formidable nature of the task of bringing about reunion, and were impatient for immediate action. The unhappy and unauthorised participation of English bishops in a Swedish Church episcopal consecration, which occurred soon after the Lambeth Conference had adjourned, affords an illustration of impulses needing to be restrained and certain to make for disorder when given the slightest seeming encouragement by high authority. It remains, of course, that the Lambeth Conference is not a legislative body. Its resolutions necessarily have great weight, and may materially affect the future legislation of Anglican Churches. But of themselves they make no action lawful for Anglican prelates which is inconsistent with the existing canon law of these Churches.

A prominent bishop of the American Church once said to me in substance, ' We have been talking so much about reunion that for the sake of consistency we ought to do something. If we are not prepared to take any steps towards reunion, we ought to stop talking.'

Undoubtedly we ought to stop the kind of talk that implies the practicability of immediate visible steps toward reunion. Work for unity, in particular between Anglicans and Nonconformists, ought for some time to be confined to educational lines, to obtaining sufficient mutual understanding and agreement in determinative principles. Talk in behalf of immediate steps toward reunion is what needs to be stopped. But the right kind of talk should go on, and should be candid and educational. The differences in questions of Faith and Order should be faced instead of being put aside, because there can be no reunion worth having until they are faced and settled in their determinative aspects. There is no call, therefore, for abandonment of conference and discussion. What is needed is to get rid of illusions, and to stop devising schemes which for the present, as between Anglicans and Nonconformist Churches, and between Catholics and Protestants in general, are abortive and interfere with real progress. These remarks do not apply, of course, to movements for reunion between Protestant Churches that differ in no particulars deemed essential by them.

CHAPTER IV

THE chief events leading up to the World Conference held at Lausanne, Switzerland, August 3–21, 1927, were a preliminary conference at Geneva in 1920, which appointed a Continuation Committee of representative nature with power to make all arrangements, and meetings of this Committee at Stockholm in 1925, at Berne in 1926, and at Lausanne on the eve of the World Conference itself. Two sub-committees—on Business and on Programme—held frequent meetings, and did efficient work. But the framing of a Programme and of Rules of Procedure satisfactory to all, and harmonising with the originally stipulated purpose and limitations of the Conference, proved to be somewhat difficult. The final outcome, however, thanks to the tactful patience of the Committee, was excellent, and registered the triumph of the original purpose and limits of the Conference. This will be made clear, I hope, as I go on.

I. *Its Appointed Aim and Business*

The aim and stipulated business of the proposed Conference was plainly indicated in the Joint Committee Report that led the American General Convention in 1910 to resolve ' That a Joint Commission be appointed to bring about a Conference for the consideration of questions touching Faith and Order, and that all Christian Communions throughout the world which confess our Lord Jesus Christ as God and Saviour be asked to unite with us in arranging for and conducting such a Conference.' This Report was sent out with the invitations to all as explaining to what kind of Conference they were invited, and each Communion which accepted the invitation was thereby committed to acceptance of the aim and limiting stipulations thus transmitted to it.

What were these stipulations?

(*a*) Its aim was to promote ' mutual understanding ' by ' the clear statement and full consideration of those things in which we differ, as well as of those things in which we are at one.'

(*b*) There was to be no throwing of convictions into solution, but we were to take part ' with loyalty to the truth as we see it ' ; and the Conference was to be limited to ' study and discussion, without power to legislate or to adopt resolutions.'

(*c*) It was to be a *World* Conference, in which the ecumenical aspects of the unity problem were to be faced. This purpose was thought by some to be defeated by Rome's refusal to participate, but to a saving degree it was preserved at Lausanne by the visibly effective influence of Orthodox Eastern and Anglican representatives. In this connection should be mentioned the Bishop of New York's brave and persuasive reminder to the assembly that the absence of Roman representatives would not justify forgetting at a World Conference the necessity of reckoning with the Roman Communion in the problem of Christian unity.

(*d*) To confer for ' study and discussion ' simply, with a view to better mutual understanding, was described as ' the next step toward unity '—next, that is, after the previous unorganised and miscellaneous efforts. These, indeed, had helped to secure general interest in the problem of unity, but had brought no progress in facing the world-wide aspects of the problem and the differences which now preclude reunion between the major bodies of Christians. Real progress would appear to require three steps : *first*, breaking up the long entrenched

D

mutual misunderstandings that now effectively hinder progress in agreement, in particular, between Catholics and Protestants ; *second*, fresh study in a new spirit of the questions of Faith and Order that must be accepted in common in any reunion that will either conform to the Lord's will or be likely to endure ; *third*, the schematic stage of uniting action. The World Conference was to be concerned with the first of these, and its success, if it succeeded, was to lie in initiating a fresh and perhaps protracted study of the questions of Faith and Order involved—a kind of study made hopeful by being based upon better mutual understanding of Christian differences.

II. *How This Aim Was Preserved*

As I have already hinted, the aim and appointed business of the Conference was not adequately or correctly understood by many. It represented a new line altogether, but was widely taken to mean merely a grandiose enlargement of the method of developing an eirenic platform which could be accepted without further ado and made the basis of legislative action looking directly to reunion, or at least to an adjustment of interdenominational relations and removal of overlapping in the religious, as well as other, activities of ' the Churches.'

(*a*) The form taken by the smaller conferences designed to prepare the way for the greater one were controlled by this mistake, notably in England ; and a series of statements of agreements were adopted by Anglicans and British Free Churchmen, published, and treated as representing progress towards unity. They were in fact ambiguous, and adopted only in mutually discordant senses. Furthermore, the assumption that, even if accepted in the same sense, they represented progress could not be admitted, in view of the absence in them of any reference to the more vital differences remaining unfaced.

The Lambeth Conference's pronouncements on unity, in spite of their evident design to preserve the Catholic standpoint, made the same dangerous assumption that sufficient agreements between Anglican and Free Churchmen might be reached in the near future to justify certain provisional irregularities pending the completion of reunion. All this helped to increase the impression that the World Conference was to aim at creating a common platform, on the basis of which schematic plans for reunion could be successfully developed. I have discussed these statements in the previous chapter.

(b) Naturally enough this impression had its effect upon those charged with framing the Programme of the Conference. In its first form, adopted by the central Continuation Committee at Stockholm, in 1925, the agenda consisted of a series of tentative propositions which the speakers at the Conference would be required to discuss, in the hope that from them would be evolved Statements of Agreement which could be unanimously adopted as 'findings' to be transmitted to the Churches. Such a programme involved shelving the appointed business of frankly facing and discussing differences, the real hindrances to unity.

Discontent was manifested in various quarters, and obtained Lutheran as well as Episcopal expression in America. On the eve of the Continuation Committee's meeting at Berne, in 1926, I sent in an appeal for substituting simple designations of topics for the suggested propositions. The Committee wisely made the substitution, but preserved the propositions in an appendix, as suggestions. The plan of controlling the Conference with a view to reaching Statements of Agreement was obviously retained. Discontent continued to be in evidence. In May 1927 I sent in to the Committee a longer memorial, in which it was argued from the official definition of the aim and scope of the Conference above described that, unless the Conference really faced, and by free discussion disembarrassed of committals sought to understand the points of difference, its appointed business would fail to be fulfilled. The memorial also gave reasons for regarding such failure as involving further delay in grappling with the real obstacles to unity. The document was sent by the Secretariat to all members of the Conference.

(c) The matter came up for settlement by the Conference with the submission for adoption of Rules of Procedure, in particular Rule 7. This rule ignored differences, but provided that no statement should be declared adopted unless accepted either unanimously or *nem. con.* It added, ' In case a statement does not gain this measure of acceptance, the Conference shall determine what further steps, if any, shall be taken on that subject.' The rule was criticised successively by Bishop Gore, myself, and Bishop Manning, and was referred to a committee for revision. Bishop Gore's amendment was designed to ' prevent statements approved merely by a large majority of the Conference from being regarded as receiving its approval.' My own objection was to the failure of the rule to secure explicit description of differences in the statements to be adopted by the Conference. The same evening our own delegation met at the call of Bishop Manning and a revised draft of the rule, embodying my contention, was adopted and transmitted as suggestion to the committee. Subsequently the chairman of the committee brought me the draft adopted by it. I did not find its language sufficiently explicit, and at his kind request suggested modifications. These modifications were accepted by the committee. The outcome was that the revised form, unanimously adopted by the Conference, required that in all reports ' any differences remaining shall be clearly indicated, as well as the agreement reached '; the requirement of unanimous or *nem. con.* acceptance was retained; but the concluding loophole for majority action was omitted.

This explicit provision for the proper business of the Conference was in due course fortified by two provisions designed to enable the Reports to be unanimously 'transmitted to the Churches,' without the members being thereby committed to any specific propositions contained in them. The *first* of these was the insertion of a clause in the Preamble of the Reports expressly exempting the members from such committal; and the *second* was a special rule providing that the votes taken on the Reports should not be for their 'adoption' but for their being 'received.' Accordingly, their unanimous transmission to the Churches does not mean 'adoption' of their propositions. Therefore it does not constitute a recommendation for their 'adoption' by the Churches. The Reports are merely registers of significant discussions, transmitted for consideration because of their educational value.

(*d*) To return to the proceedings of the Conference. Seven subjects were dealt with, beginning in each case with a day of appointed papers and addresses. Subject I, 'The Call of Unity,' received no further discussion. In the cases of Subject II, 'The Church's Message to the World—the Gospel'; III, 'The Nature of the Church'; and IV, 'The Church's Common Confession of Faith,' the appointed addresses were followed by as many impromptu speeches (limited to ten minutes for the speech *and* its interpretation into the other two languages used) as the rest of the day permitted. Then the Conference was divided into three sections, each concerned with one of the three subjects, and each section was broken into groups of about twenty members each—care being taken to have every principal standpoint represented in each section and group. Each group reported agreements and differences to its section, and the section as a whole, by discussion and reference to a drafting committee, built up a Report which was subsequently presented to the whole Conference, there being again discussed, amended, referred to a general drafting committee, and finally voted on.

The same procedure was adopted with Subjects V,

'The Church's Ministry'; VI, 'The Sacraments'; and VII, 'The Unity of Christendom and the Relation thereto of existing Churches,' except that all discussion of the appointed addresses was relegated to the sections and sub-groups.

The result was that the Chairman's draft of the Preamble and Statement on Subject I were 'adopted' unanimously. The Reports on Subjects II–VI as finally whipped into shape were 'received'—not 'adopted'—*nem. con.* for transmission to the Churches. All the Reports thus 'received' indicated differences as well as agreements; and the Preamble explicitly disclaimed for the members of the Conference any committal to specific statements in these Reports.

The Report on Subject VII, 'The Unity of Christendom and the Relation thereto of existing Churches,' proved unacceptable for any form of transmission to the Churches. It really lay beyond the appointed scope of the Conference, was Protestant in outlook, and failed clearly to indicate the differences. Because time to bring it into line with the other Reports was lacking, and the Conference wished to avoid breaking the record of *nem. con.* voting, it was received for reference to the Continuation Committee without instructions. This Committee subsequently revised it and published it in the revised form —somewhat improved, but even so not a document that the Conference would have been able to receive *nem. con.* In any case, such reception of it has not taken place.

III. *Incidental Matters*

(*a*) Several unique aspects of the Conference should be noted. *First* of all, it was the first instance, since the breakup of the sixteenth century, of representatives of all types of Christians except Roman meeting, with friendly intent, to reckon frankly with their differences. That fact alone gives the Conference important historical significance, and reveals a new spirit.

Secondly, with much earnest prayer and a sense of being peculiarly under divine prompting, the members of the Conference listened patiently to those with whom they most acutely disagreed, and strove to understand sympathetically ideas that had hitherto been viewed in fog-banks of controversy and caricature. The exhibition of mutual friendliness in the midst of the bluntest frankness on inflammatory subjects was simply a marvel of divine grace. Every emergence of polemic was quickly absorbed in the all-pervading determination for mutual kindness and respect. Accordingly, there was a joyous but friendly freedom of speech which, all things considered, probably stands alone in human history.

But *thirdly*, the spirit of compromise for the sake of peace, with its accompaniment of diplomatic ambiguities and make-believe agreements, was excluded with the utmost determination by Catholic and Protestant alike. Ambiguities did unavoidably appear in the Reports ; but, as I have shown, the Conference took pains not to ' adopt ' them.

A deep sense of stewardship for the several conceptions of Christian Faith and Order to which they gave witness was plainly controlling most of the members. Modern Liberalism did gain some expression, even in the Reports, but it was completely overshadowed by frequent firm enunciations of the necessity of faithfulness to the historic Faith. This was especially apparent in the discussions on the Catholic Creeds ; and Lutherans and Presbyterians bore testimony along with Orthodox Easterns and Anglicans to the necessity of a dogmatic faith. Such an atmosphere, when it pervades Christendom, will materially hasten the triumph of truth—of the Church's ancient Faith and Order.

(*b*) A few words on the attitude of the Orthodox Easterns, whose refusal to vote at all, except for the Preamble and for the Report on the Gospel Message, has been published in a sensational and misleading way. While refusing to vote for Reports III–VI, on account of their miscellaneous contents, they refrained from voting against them, thus enabling them to be received *nemine contradicente*. They made a loving explanation of their course, and explicitly retained their membership of the Conference and representation in the new Continuation Committee elected by the Conference. The best of feeling was preserved. Their action accentuated the policy of exempting the members of the Conference from committal to specific statements in the Reports, but did not create this policy. It had been practically determined before their pronouncement was made, and had the support of Protestant as well as Catholic members of the Conference.

(*c*) The expressed desire of certain members to commit the Conference to such schemes as the interchange of pulpits and occasional intercommunion—so dear to those within the Anglican Communion who fail to realise the compromising and disturbing effects of such irregularities—was simply out of serious reckoning. Their promoters perceived that the matter could not safely be pressed to a vote.

(*d*) The Continuation Committee, charged with carrying on the Conference movement, was made much more truly representative of every section. Its plans will no doubt develop gradually. If in accord with the mind of the Conference at large, they will preserve its educational and non-committal policy. Another World Conference may meet some day, but practical possibilities and obvious wisdom are against hurry in the matter.

IV. *Concluding Argument*

That the Lausanne Conference scored a very notable *immediate* success is too apparent to be denied by those who have correct knowledge of what it did and of what it avoided doing. But this means only that it succeeded in fulfilling its appointed business of promoting mutual understanding of the differences in Faith and Order which have to be faced in effective labour for world-wide unity. That is, it means success in initiating an educational method which must be continued for some time in order to bring forth visible fruit.

It should be noted that the World Conference was intended to enable its participants to consider questions of Faith and Order ' in ecumenical light,' that is, in view of the need and requirements of *world-wide* reunion. And it became apparent at Lausanne that a vast majority of Christians retain the ancient Catholic Faith and Order as being of divine appointment and ' incapable of compromise or surrender.' Moreover, entrenched in a well-fortified tradition of many centuries, they are not likely to modify this position in any future which we can anticipate. Whatever we may think, therefore, as to the merits of their attitude, it constitutes a major fact to reckon with in promoting the reunion of Christendom at large. Nothing less than such reunion can achieve the unity of the one flock for which Christ prayed ; and to many Anglicans no scheme of union with particular sections of Christendom is tolerable that will sacrifice any integral element of ancient Catholic Faith and Order, and thus make this major consummation more difficult and remote.

It is in the light of this situation that we should regard the attitude of those earnest leaders, in and out of the Anglican Communion, who think that with sufficient love, skill, and courage the barriers to reunion, at least outside the Roman and Eastern Orthodox Churches, can be broken down in this generation. Whatever may be possible as between Protestant Churches, the only means by which reunion between Protestant and Anglican Churches can be had, without causing schism among Anglicans, is a return of Protestants ' to the principles of unity exemplified by the undivided Catholic Church during the first ages of its existence.' It is as impossible to commit an *undivided* Anglican Communion to reunion on any other basis as it is thus to commit the Roman and

Eastern Orthodox Communions. It is also true, of course, that this return to ancient principles must not involve a return to the later corruptions and tyrannies which caused the sixteenth-century revolt.

The work at Lausanne, wonderful as it was, had pioneer limitations; and some of the most central questions requiring settlement before ecumenical reunion can become practical politics were left undiscussed. The rest of this book will deal with the more critical ones. But their consideration will be introduced by a chapter giving a comprehensive survey of the requirements which apparently will have to be reckoned with somehow in bringing about the reunion of all Christendom.

CHAPTER V

REQUIREMENTS FOR REUNION

ADHERING as faithfully as I can to the ecumenical point of view, I shall not seek in this chapter to ventilate or defend personal views, but to *lay bare the situation and to bring out the largeness of the problem of reunion.*

I have given reasons in previous chapters for assuming : (*a*) that nothing short of the corporate union of all Christian Communions fully agrees with the mind of Christ ; (*b*) that all smaller unions, and all schemes and arrangements leading thereto, should be consistent with progress towards this goal ; (*c*) that no schematic action should be taken which is likely to create new obstacles to the final reunion of Christendom.

A really fresh and co-operative study of certain principles of Faith and Order embodied in the historic Catholic system is needed—not less for professed adherents to that system than for those who have rejected vital elements of it. Unwarranted accretions and reactionary mutilations have equally to be reconsidered. Roman theologians, on the one hand, have to consider whether the Vatican claims for the Papal See, and distinctively Roman teachings and practices, are really integral to the primacy which the ancient Church recognised, and to the primitive Faith and Order at large. Protestant theologians, on the other hand, should reopen the question whether, *in their proper nature*, certain Catholic principles are to be identified with, or necessarily involve, the corrupt conceptions and practices rightly rejected in the sixteenth century.

I. *In General*

By ' requirements ' I do not here mean ' terms,' or specific proposals the acceptance of which will be required on the Catholic side as a formal basis of reunion. I doubt the possibility of accurately anticipating what terms in this sense will ultimately be stipulated in reunion either between Catholic and Nonconformist bodies or between bodies within one of these groups. It is quite possible that, when the conditions for ecumenical reunion have sufficiently developed for final action, a common mind and purpose will have emerged that will very materially reduce the formidableness of the ' terms ' exacted by the several parties to such reunion. I am seeking to summarise principles of Faith and Order which are regarded by the larger section of Christendom as integral to Christianity. And they are maintained with varying degrees of articulate definition and emphasis by a body of Anglicans sufficiently influential, and sufficiently fortified by ecclesiastical formularies and prescriptions, to determine how far the Anglican Communion can go in the interest of reunion with Nonconformists.

Two significant Anglican pronouncements will serve as convenient introduction.

1. The first Lambeth Conference declared, ' We . . . do hereby solemnly record our conviction that unity will be most effectually promoted by maintaining the Faith in its purity and integrity, as taught in the Holy Scriptures, held by the Primitive Church, summed up in the Creeds, and affirmed by the undisputed General Councils.'

2. The American House of Bishops, in the main part of its Declaration on Unity, which has been widely and misleadingly ignored in interpreting the ' Quadrilateral ' appended thereto, says, ' We do hereby affirm that the Christian Unity now so earnestly desired . . . can be restored only by the return of all Christian Communions to the principles of unity exemplified by the undivided

Catholic Church during the first ages of its existence ; which principles we believe to be the substantial deposit of Christian Faith and Order committed by Christ and His Apostles to the Church unto the end of the world, and therefore incapable of compromise or surrender by those who have been ordained to be its stewards and trustees for the common and equal benefit of all men.' The four articles of the ' Quadrilateral,' appended as examples of what was meant, including ' the Historic Episcopate,' were explicitly described as ' inherent parts of this sacred deposit.'   The contention that the Historic Episcopate was included merely as an ancient fact, without any particular view of its origin, is therefore plainly mistaken, although the Bishops did declare the need of its being ' locally adapted in the methods of its administration to the varying needs of the nations and peoples called of God into the unity of His Church.' I have already said this, but it will bear repetition.

My general thesis is that, among the questions of Faith and Order that have to be faced and patiently studied by all who labour for world-wide reunion, the leading ones are raised by the belief of a vast majority of Christendom that the ancient Catholic system—I do not mean anything peculiarly Roman— comes from Christ, and therefore is the only available basis of complete and permanent Christian unity.

I would here remark that this is not a personal theory, but an obvious situation—one that cannot be disregarded in really intelligent work for unity. The particular requirements that I am to indicate may seem distinctively Anglo-Catholic, but their practical urgency in the reunion problem lies in their having had many centuries of general consent, and in their still retaining the consent of seven-tenths of Christendom.   They are not *peculiarly* Anglo-Catholic. Protestants surely ought to reckon with this fact, and therefore not hastily to decline the task of investigating freshly and patiently the questions involved.

II. *Intrinsic*

The requirements of ecumenical union may be classified in two groups : (*a*) those that are involved in a general restoration of the Faith and Order permanently committed to the Church by Christ and His Apostles, purified, of course, of all corrupting accretions ; (*b*) those that pertain to securing and maintaining in the reunited Church such degree of mutual conformity in other matters as will be needed if a common spiritual atmosphere and mutual understanding are to be preserved. In brief, the requirements are partly intrinsic and partly extrinsic—the former not admitting of compromise, the latter susceptible of modification by common consent, and of elastic adjustment in details to times, places, and conditions. In this section I seek to indicate the more fundamental, intrinsic requirements, as Oriental, Roman, and Anglican Catholics alike regard them.

(*a*) Practical acceptance of the whole historic Faith, as taught by the ancient Catholic Church, as partly defined in the Catholic Creeds, and as confirmed by the Scriptures. This requires that the supernatural shall not be so interpreted as to subvert their historic meaning. On the other hand, it leaves Christians free either to accept or to reject theological and popular opinions not provably involved in the Faith, and fearlessly to welcome all additions to knowledge gained by human inquiry. However, such knowledge ought not to be understood to enlarge or alter in substance the doctrines once for all revealed for guidance into eternal life, but simply to enrich the intelligence with which we receive, defend, and apply them.

(*b*) The teaching authority of the universal Church should be acknowledged. This does not mean that mental freedom and private judgment should be abandoned. A faith that does not represent personal persuasion is defective. It means that, in the exercise of

such freedom, men are to reckon with Christ's commission to His Church and His promise that it should be
guided by the Holy Spirit. Waiving aside contentious
infallibilist terms, His commission should be recognised
as making the Faith of the universal Church quite the
most weighty, authoritative, and dependable definition to
Christian believers of saving doctrine that can be had on
earth. The fact that those who treat the Scriptures as
the sole Rule of Faith are not led thereby to adequate
consent in doctrine, and the contrasted fact that those
who accept the Church's teaching authority are agreed
much more comprehensively therein, and so agreed in
spite of centuries of schism between Catholic bodies,
these facts should suggest to Protestants a fresh consideration of the whole subject. And it should be
remembered that the teaching authority of the Church
does not in Catholic judgment do away with the necessity
that Church doctrine should stand the test of confirmation
by Scripture.

(c) The ancient sacramentalism of the Church should
be accepted both doctrinally and practically as a vital
element of the Christian system. An increasing number
of critical scholars find it in St. Paul's Epistles, and the
attempt to prove that in this St. Paul departed from Christ
is futile. It needs to be agreed for reunion that the
sacraments are appointed instruments of supernatural
operations of the Holy Spirit. They are not beneficial
except under moral conditions, certainly not to the
unbelieving and impenitent ; but their objective efficacy
as means of grace is due to the pledged, specific, and
supernatural operation in them of the Holy Spirit—not
to our faith. The primary sacraments, of course, are
Baptism and the Holy Communion, but if we are to use
the term sacrament in the traditional sense of any
appointed means of sanctifying grace, the sacramental
requirements of unity cannot be restricted to these two.
The laying on of hands, or Confirmation, is plainly
treated in the New Testament as the prescribed means by

which the gifts of the Holy Spirit are bestowed upon the baptised. The sacrament of Penance is simply the generally appointed method by which the ministers of Christ exercise the authority which He gave them of remitting sins in His Name. Ordination in the New Testament is clearly treated as imparting the Holy Spirit for the work of the ministry. The Catholic Church cannot without betrayal of trust permit these things to be treated as admitting of compromise in the interests of unity.

Moreover, Catholics will insist that Baptism be regarded as the appointed means of admission to the Church, of incorporation into Christ's Body, and consequently of participation in His supernatural sonship. This last is the meaning of baptismal regeneration as maintained by Catholics. If they used the term regeneration to signify personal conversion, they would of course admit that infants are not regenerate in Baptism.

Finally, although considerable theological liberty and provincial variation can be discovered in Catholic views of the Holy Communion, and such liberty will surely remain in the reunited Catholic Church, certain requirements will beyond doubt be treated as not open to compromise : (i) that the consecrated species, in a mysterious but not less real and vital sense, are the Body and Blood of Christ ; (ii) that as the appointed memorial before God of Christ's death, and the means whereby we plead its merits and in union with Christ formally and corporately offer ourselves to God, it is sacrificial ; (iii) that, as in New Testament days, it should be the central act of Christian worship on every Lord's Day at least, with such regular frequency of communion by individuals as their spiritual states permit.

(d) The ancient threefold ministry of bishops, priests, and deacons will have to be recognised in the reunited Church, and Catholic doctrine will not permit its permanence to be made uncertain by its authority being based upon mere human compact. To the Catholic mind it represents Orders that have been appointed by the Holy Spirit, and that depend for their assured continuance upon unbroken succession by means of episcopal ordination. The difficulty of Protestant scholars in accepting this conviction seems largely to be due to their not reckoning adequately with certain outstanding and determinative facts, and to their absorption in the apparently impossible task of clearly tracing the ministerial developments of the obscure period of, say, seventy-five years after St. Paul's death. It is to be admitted that the data available for this period are too fragmentary for formal proof of what is meant by the modern phrase ' apostolic succession '; but they are also too fragmentary for disproof, and the state of the question among those who survived that period, and lived in the last half of the second century, is therefore to be reckoned with.

The outstanding established facts are : (i) that Christ established the apostolate as the beginning of the ministry with which He promised to abide until the end of the world ; (ii) that while this ministry was reinforced for the emergencies of the creative period by prophets especially raised up, for the normal ordering of the mother Church of Jerusalem the apostolic ministry was differentiated into three grades—James, the presbyters, and the deacons ; (iii) that when the sub-apostolic Church emerged into clear historical light, this threefold ministry was found to be generally accepted as having divinely guided apostolic appointment—and this before the tradition of apostolic arrangements had had time to become unreliable in its main substance; (iv) that during the intervening period, the missionary Churches were not given self-sufficient organisation, their ministers having only the Orders of presbyters (also called bishops because charged with local oversight) and deacons ; but that ordinations, so far as recorded, were performed by ministers of higher rank, e.g. St. Paul and his delegates, Timothy and Titus. No exclusively presbyterial or congregational ordination has been proved to have occurred,

or to have been treated as sufficient, in the primitive
Church. To Catholic scholars these facts appear to
determine the state of the question, and to show that the
broad stream of tradition *ad rem* should be accepted until
its falsity has been proved. This surely has not been
done. Such facts as have been alleged, neither numerous
nor usually free from obscurity, appear susceptible of
interpretation in harmony with the traditional doctrine.

In considering the Historic Episcopate, it should be
remembered that the various abuses summed up in the
word ' prelacy,' and rightly condemned by Protestants,
do not inhere in episcopacy as such, but grew out of the
secularisation of the Church through its relation to the
State and its resulting civil status and privilege. This
abuse can and must be guarded against in the reunited
Church.

(*e*) The perpetuation of the ministerial priesthood,
always treated in Catholic doctrine as an essential
element of the Christian system, is one of the leading
reasons for insisting upon the episcopate. A lively
memory of offensive sacerdotal abuses naturally makes it
difficult for Protestants patiently to consider this subject
afresh, and to realise that the most acute objections to
' sacerdotalism ' do not rightly apply to the Catholic
doctrine of priesthood but to reformable abuses. None
the less, the whole subject has to be faced, and patiently
reckoned with, if world-wide Christian unity is to be
attained.

I have space for only a few remarks on this
troublesome subject. According to Catholic doctrine,
ministerial priests constitute a distinct sacred Order in
the Church, and their characteristic functions—*e.g.* in
the Eucharist and in the ministry of reconciliation—
cannot be validly performed except by those who have
been admitted to the priestly Order by episcopal ordination. That mediæval abuses had deplorable effect is of
course true. But that the appointed exercise of the
sacerdotal functions above referred to involves an inter-

vention between the individual soul and God which deprives the laity of free access to Him, and trenches upon Christ's sole mediatorship, is not borne out by the normal experience of devout Catholics. Moreover, if, as Catholics believe, the ministerial priesthood is of divine appointment, the remedy for its human abuses is not an abandonment of priesthood but their reformation.

Two lines of study, carefully pursued, ought to be helpful in clarifying the whole subject. The *first* is suggested by the Catholic doctrine that the ministerial priesthood represents the manner in which Christ—the real operator, through His Spirit, in the sacraments—accommodates the earthly exercise of His mediatorial office to our conditions and limitations. The earthly priesthood is Christ's own hand, so to speak, extended to us. The *second* is the doctrine of the Church as the Body of Christ —an organism, and therefore possessed of organs through which the *whole body* operates. The organ—the priest— is not external to the body, and cannot act apart from its other members. The relation between priest and people is interior, and the whole body shares by corporate participation in what the ministerial priest does ministerially and as organ of the body.

To conclude this section, however imperfect my expositions may be, it is certain that in fundamental substance the requirements here described are regarded throughout Catholic Christendom as integral elements of Christianity and insusceptible of material compromise. And this fact has to be reckoned with in every actual step towards reunion in which the Anglican communion can take part without internal disruption.

III. *Extrinsic*

I come now to the requirements which pertain to effectiveness of the unity that we aim to establish. This unity involves not only the fundamentals of Faith and Order, but requires one universal and corporate fellowship in sacramental life and worship, recognisable by all participants and visible to the world. Nothing short of this can fulfil Christ's prayer for the oneness of His disciples and correspond to the teachings of St. Paul as seen in 1 Corinthians xii. and Ephesians iv. This means, of course, schematic agreement as to the human arrangements by which, in the reunited Christendom, the balance between authority and freedom will be kept practically secure and all Christians will find themselves at home wherever in all the world they may travel. Being human, these arrangements will be subject to a considerable degree of adaptation to local conditions. None the less, if the common fellowship is effectively to be safeguarded, there will have to be general conformity in certain obtrusively significant externals of corporate practice. It would be premature to define them narrowly. I attempt only to indicate summarily and tentatively what appear to be their more obvious lines.

(*a*) If the Church is to be visibly one throughout the world, it would seem that no other distributions of ecclesiastical jurisdiction and governmental autonomy should be retained than are essential to effective local ordering of Christian interests. The continuance of ' Churches ' of obtrusively divergent methods of Christian regimen is not consistent with the effective common fellowship that is required. Particular needs may indeed continue to be cherished by unofficial societies, orders, or guilds ; but for them to assume denominational standing, so as to differentiate Christians in corporate worship and discipline, is surely prejudicial to unity, since it must hinder the development of a common spiritual life.

(*b*) In the balance between conformity and freedom that will be needed, the requirements of general conformity will naturally centre in Eucharistic worship and sacramental ministrations. The importance that has ever been attached to their safeguarding—to their visibly retaining for ever their original appointed meaning and application—will preclude Catholic acceptance of doctrinally significant divergence in their ministration. The Eucharistic Liturgies of Catholic Churches everywhere, varying as they do in many details, are sufficiently alike to be recognised as having a common norm and meaning. It will surely be required that this norm shall not be significantly violated in any part of the reunited Catholic Church, and that, as in primitive days, Eucharistic worship shall be the central corporate function of at least every Lord's Day. This alone can provide the necessary rallying point of Christians in their corporate approach to God.

(c) On the other hand, outside the sacramental sphere there must be a very considerable degree of liberty, both in local adaptations of episcopal polity and in public services. That the principle of uniformity has been pushed too far in Anglican history is clearly evident. Outside the common Eucharistic worship there should be explicit allowance of any diversity that is consistent with Christian principles and decent order. Prayer Meetings, Experience Meetings, Revivals, Missions, Retreats, Quiet Days, Meditations, and all forms of congregational exercises that are found to be edifying, and are not conducted with divisive aim, should be freely conceded to the discretion of local pastors and congregations. None of these services—I include Morning and Evening Prayer —should be so prescribed for all as to preclude deviation for common edification and to meet varying local, congregational, or missionary needs and exigencies. Conformity should not mean a uniformity prejudicial to decent liberty and spiritual enthusiasm.

(d) These things, it is clear, cannot be ordered in effective unity without some continuing ccumcnical machinery ; and agreement as to its nature, powers, and limitations cannot be had without reckoning with the Roman primacy, its sanctions, its implications and limits, and the safeguards against renewal of past excesses, upon the acceptance of which by the Roman See its continued primacy in the reunited Church will surely depend. The subject is too large and contentious to be handled in this chapter; and such treatment of it as is practicable in this volume will be found in the later chapter on ' Authority and Freedom.'

CHAPTER VI

THE MINISTRY

In undertaking to reckon with the leading questions raised by the ecumenical requirements for Reunion as I have tried to define them in the previous chapter, I shall not observe their logical order, but rather the order in which they have emerged in discussions between Anglicans and Nonconformists. Therefore I consider at once the question of the ministry.

I. *Various Positions*

According to the Catholic doctrine, the ministry of bishops, priests, and deacons was instituted under the guidance of the Holy Spirit by the Apostles and may not lawfully be abandoned by human authority so long as this world lasts. It is part of this doctrine also that the power of ordaining men to this ministry has been given from apostolic days exclusively to the first of these orders. Such has been the doctrine generally held, and practically observed, until the Protestant revolt of the sixteenth century; and it is still adhered to by the major part of Christendom. The Preface of the Anglican Ordinal plainly expresses it, and refuses to acknowledge those lacking episcopal ordination ' as ministers of this Church.' Our American House of Bishops, in its Declaration on Unity of 1886, also specified ' the Historic Episcopate ' as one of the ' parts ' of the ' substantial deposit of Christian Faith and Order committed by Christ and His Apostles to the Church unto the end of the world, and therefore incapable of compromise or surrender.'

Over against this are several contrary positions dating from the sixteenth century. The Swedish Church has preserved technically the episcopal succession; but treats it as non-essential, and has suppressed the diaconate. An important section of Presbyterians profess to believe in apostolic succession, but claim to have preserved it in the presbyterate. All Presbyterians believe, of course, in the validity of presbyterial ordination. The Congregationalists definitely reject the need of apostolic succession in the usual sense of that phrase, and hold each congregation to possess full power as to the manner of admitting men to the ministry.

II. *Recent Conferences*

The Lambeth Conference of 1920 went as far as Catholic principles permitted in making concessions on this subject. Indeed, as the event proved, some of its language was open to misconstruction. It thankfully acknowledged that non-episcopal ministries ' have been manifestly blessed and owned by the Holy Spirit as effective means of grace.' It also made the following proposal. For an approach to union, ' we who send forth this appeal would say that if the authorities of other Communions so desire, we are persuaded that, terms of union having been otherwise satisfactorily adjusted, bishops and clergy of our Communion would willingly accept from these authorities a form of commission or recognition which would commend our ministry to their congregations as having its place in the one family life. . . . It is our hope that the same motive would lead ministers who have not received it to accept a commission through episcopal ordination, as obtaining for them a ministry throughout the whole fellowship. In so acting no one of us could possibly be taken to repudiate his past ministry. . . . Nor would any of us be dishonouring the Holy Spirit of God, whose call led us all to our several ministries, and whose power enabled us to perform them.'

In subsequent conferences between representatives of the English Free Churches and of the Church of England, the former rejected the idea of submitting to episcopal ordination as inconsistent with the validity of their previous non-episcopal ordination—this validity having been proved by many evidences of spiritual blessing. They acknowledged, however, that for practical reasons the episcopate ought to be accepted 'for the United Church of the future,' 'as the means whereby the authority of the whole body is given.' But they said that for them this 'would not imply the reception of any particular theory as to its origin or character, or the disowning of past ministries of the Word and Sacrament otherwise received.'

The Anglican representatives tentatively suggested hypothetical ordination, as meeting Catholic requirements without involving reflection on previous ministerial status. Nothing came of this. The Anglicans also made the statement 'that the ministries which we have in view . . . which imply a sincere intention to preach Christ's Word and administer the Sacraments as Christ has ordained, and to which authority so to do has been solemnly given by the Church concerned, are real ministries of Christ's Word and Sacraments in the Universal Church.' They had just said, 'Such Free Church ministries we find it impossible to regard as " invalid," that is, null and void, or as effecting none of the purposes for which the ministry has been Divinely ordained in the Church of Christ. Indeed, we wish that the terms " valid " and " invalid " could be discontinued, involving as they seem to do a knowledge of the Divine Will and purpose which we do not possess, and which it would be presumption to claim.'

This last statement reveals a mistake as to the Catholic

use of the terms ' valid ' and ' invalid.' Rightly used, a
valid ministry or sacrament means one in which the
divine arrangements for the Church's ministry and
sacraments are fully conformed to. Whether God will
bless ' invalid ' ministrations when employed with sincere
loyalty to Christ, is a different question. Anglicans of
every school have frequently acknowledged that God has
blessed non-episcopal ministrations, even when denying
their validity, that is, their full conformity to the divine
appointments for the Church.

The acknowledgment above quoted that non-episcopal
ministries are ' real ministries of Christ's Word and
Sacraments in the Universal Church,' is with difficulty
susceptible of Catholic interpretation, and was taken by
the Free Churches' representatives as logically pointing
to unqualified recognition of Protestant ministries and to
action along the lines of exchange of pulpits, of communion, and of recognition that Protestant Churches *as
such* are corporate parts of the Catholic Church. The
Anglican representatives were constrained to explain that
' spiritual efficacy is one thing, due authority is another.
The latter is not involved in the former. The full
admission which we have most readily made . . . does
not carry with it the admission that they have due
authority.' They add the significant words, ' But we
regard this bestowal of authority of the whole body to
the Ministry by Episcopal Ordination not merely as
something which is desirable for the united Church of
the future, but as something which from the Apostles'
time has always been provided for the Church. We see
in this provision a token of the guidance of the Church
by the Holy Spirit and of the Divine purpose. We
regard the acceptance of it as a trust to which the Anglican
Church is called to be faithful.'

It having become apparent that differences of view
remained which a continuance of discussion was unlikely
to remove, the conferences were suspended, pending
further study. I venture the comment that, in their

effort to reach all possible terms of agreement with Nonconformists, the Anglicans, and the same is true of the Lambeth Conference, fell into misleading ambiguities. And the inferences inevitably drawn from some of their expressions were not such as can be reconciled with the official position and established prescriptions of the Anglican Communion. The language last quoted indicates that the Anglican representatives became conscious of this ; and they felt driven to add these words, *' For our endeavour is not merely to meet difficulties and restore unity in our own country, but to do this in such a way as may form a basis for still wider union throughout the world. However remote the attainment of such an ideal may seem, we are responsible for seeing that nothing which we do now will create a new obstacle to that attainment'* (italics mine). In these words they took the ecumenical standpoint—the standpoint which controls the arguments of this volume, and is alone consistent with real advance toward the reunion of all Christendom.

When viewed from this standpoint, it is evident that the threefold ministry of bishops, priests, and deacons must retain its ancient place everywhere in reunited Christendom ; and that if by a combination of episcopal, presbyterial, and congregational polities is meant any exception to the spiritual control or pastorate to be exercised by this ministry, it cannot be accepted by the reunited Church. It should be added that the spiritual interests and just liberties for which the presbyterial and congregational polities stand will suffer no reduction, but will be guarded in juster proportion by the threefold ministry referred to when it has obtained that measure of reformation that will undoubtedly precede or attend ecumenical reunion.

I venture a further confident opinion. The major part of Christendom maintains the threefold ministry on the ground that it is divinely appointed, and cannot reasonably be expected to shift the basis of its acceptance to mere human compact, open to modification. I do not mean that this doctrine of divine appointment will necessarily have to be subscribed to in a formal way. The Catholic Churches do not require separate subscription to every doctrine. I mean that any formal disclaimer of this doctrine will surely raise a barrier to reunion in Catholic judgment.

III. *The Appeal to History*

The fact has to be reckoned with in this connection that much recent inquiry by scholarly experts has resulted in denial : (*a*) that the threefold ministry is of apostolic prescription ; (*b*) that the doctrine of apostolic succession in the modern sense of that phrase can be found in the earlier Christian Fathers. If these denials have really been made good, the Catholic doctrine on the subject requires modification. I say modification rather than reversal. It would still remain true that the peaceful development and crystallisation of the threefold ministry in every part of the Church, along with acceptance of an inflexible rule of episcopal ordination, points to an over-ruling providence—one that is too evident to be disregarded—especially by a minority of Christendom. Granted that the revolt of the sixteenth century was provoked by intolerable abuses of the Catholic hierarchy, it can still be maintained with reason that the basis of reunion should be *reform* of the hierarchy *and restoration* to its ancient status as thus reformed.

I can make no reasonable claim to rival the scholars referred to in minute investigation of the data upon which they base their negative conclusions. I am, however, fortified by the researches of men like Lightfoot, Gore, Turner, and R. C. Moberly, and especially by considering what I believe to be the erroneous method usually employed in studying the origin of the episcopate. This method has been to marshal the confessedly fragmentary data of the period following, say, the death of St. Paul, and upon their basis exclusively to determine their conclusion—'not proven.' Of course not! But neither do the data disprove the traditional doctrine, for they are, and have been shown to be, susceptible of interpretation in harmony with it. The truth is that, if the subsequently emerging Catholic tradition is disregarded, the evidence as to the origin of the Catholic ministry is too fragmentary to justify either Catholic or Protestant conclusions; and to insist upon disregarding the broad stream of early Catholic tradition is to preclude reaching any conclusion that can rightly claim finality. A similar disregard of tradition would leave us without sufficient basis for acceptance of the New Testament Canon.

The narrow scrutiny which hinders from seeing the wood for the trees needs to be widened. Scholars need in matters of inadequate contemporary evidence to reckon with the earliest clear state of the question, and with that in mind to consider whether such contemporary data as are available can be reasonably interpreted in harmony with it. And the earliest state of the question is the broad stream of tradition which is found in secure possession at the earliest period of which we can obtain dependable and sufficient knowledge. This tradition is a significant datum in any case, for it represents the closest approximation to determinative contemporary witness concerning apostolic arrangements for the ministry which can now be had—a witness which for true scholarship should be taken as holding the field until convincing contrary evidence is discovered. The burden of proof is certainly on those who reject the Catholic tradition. This tradition appears to be already existing when the Church still had among its leaders men who had been immediate recipients of apostolic teaching. To insist that it determines the initial state of the question—the burden of proof—may indeed be done in an unhappy partisan spirit, but is none the less a requirement of scholarly method of inquiry. On the other hand, to disregard the tradition in the interest of freedom from bias may indeed be done, has been done, with scholarly intent, but hardly with success in avoiding bias.

According to this tradition, the beginnings of which antedate the earliest period of which we have determinate knowledge of the ancient belief concerning the ministry, the Apostles arranged before their departure for the continuance of the ministerial oversight, the norm thereof being the threefold ministry established in Jerusalem. It is true that for obvious prudential reasons the missionary Churches were not at first given autonomous equipment, and their resident overseers, the Pastoral Epistles being witness, were without power to ordain. Ordinations were performed by visitors with apostolic powers. But as fast as these Churches became autonomous, their organisation is seen to conform to the Jerusalem norm, the overwhelming presumption being that the method of the transition did not violate the rule that ordinations should be performed by men with apostolic powers. This rule was recognised, as far back as the matter can be traced, as absolute, and cases of non-episcopal ordination accepted by the Church have not been discovered.

These facts are of determinative implication; and, while they leave many details for investigation, in the absence of undeniable proof to the contrary, they seem to bear out the Catholic tradition. Its leading particulars are: (a) the threefold ministry of bishops, priests, and deacons is of apostolic arrangement and prescription; (b) ordination, in this arrangement, can be performed only by members of the highest of these Orders. It should be added that these apostolic arrangements were justly believed to be divinely guided.

It is true that the phrase 'apostolic succession' in its present use is modern, and that when the ancients spoke of episcopal succession they meant succession in sees. But the inflexible law requiring that ordinations should be performed by bishops establishes the fact of which the modern phrase 'apostolic succession' is the description. And recent discussion has sufficiently shown that the peculiar method of succession in the Alexandrian See need not be interpreted to have been an exception to the requirement of episcopal ordination.

IV. *Corruptions to be Reformed*

I have not been trying in the last section to make a full examination of the data discussed in recent treatises on the early ministry of the Church.   I have simply tried to show that, unless the early tradition on the subject, and certain outstanding facts agreeing therewith, are more adequately reckoned with than certain recent scholars have reckoned with them, their analytical skill will not be productive of conclusions which can abide.

The data which I have given—all readily verifiable—point to apostolic origin of the Catholic form of the ministry and to the necessity of episcopal ordination for its perpetuation.   Moreover, it is reasonable to hold, as did the ancient Church, that in so central a matter, and in view of the accepted postulate that *God* has set the ministers in His Church, the Apostles acted with the authority of the Holy Spirit in making arrangements for the continuation of the oversight.   Clement of Rome claims that they were forewarned to do so by the Lord Himself.

However, episcopacy is not exempt from corruption and need of reformation.   In its corrupt state it is stigmatised as ' prelacy,' which stands with show of reason for worldly ambition, general secularity, and related things which obscure the spiritual pastorate proper to episcopacy and alienate many souls.

The reality of the difficulty I acknowledge, and it would be useless to engage in controversy on the subject.   None the less, the interests of reunion, which plainly cannot be had without an acceptance of the episcopate by all Christendom, constrain me to submit the following considerations which I believe non-episcopalians ought carefully and patiently to weigh.

(*a*) Granting that reforms are still needed, I think it is clear that the episcopate has greatly improved spiritually even in the Roman Communion since the sixteenth century, and is still gaining in truly Christian efficiency. Therefore, its state at the time of the Reformation ought not at all to be treated as determining what its future acceptance by Protestants is likely to involve. The Church militant, being made up of human beings, will never be free from evils; but corruptions that have been recovered from are not apt to recur on the same lines. History does not repeat itself.

(*b*) Even at its worst, the episcopate has preserved an external Order in the Church under which many millions of common folk, and many intelligent people as well, have been enabled to draw near to Christ and to find their way home to God. At its best, the episcopate has been a mighty force for spiritual ends, and at its worst it has been unable wholly to defeat them.

(*c*) The past secularisation of the episcopate, including the monarchical development of the Roman See, was largely due to the entangling alliance with the State which the Emperor Constantine inaugurated. Out of this grew the secular powers and jurisdictions obtained by popes and bishops, and these practically had to develop in the way they did before their hopeless inconsistency with spiritual pastorate could become clearly apparent. The ultimate completion of reformation apparently requires entire abolition everywhere of mixture between civil and ecclesiastical authority. I personally believe that there should be world-wide ' disestablishment ' and spiritual disentanglement of the Church, which should have no part in civil affairs beyond those forms of *persuasion* in public moral issues which all subjects of the State ought to be free to exercise. The Church is, of course, entitled as a voluntary society to hold property, and to have its property rights protected by the State; but no more so than any other corporation. Church and State, as such, must be mutually independent, if the Church is to escape a chief cause of secularity and ' prelacy,' and is to be able to legislate spiritually without external obstruction.

(d) The demand for constitutionalising the episcopate is just in so far as it means what Catholics call ' canon law,' amended by ecumenical consent in such wise as definitely to protect the inferior clergy and laity in the rights which they ought to have under Christ, to limit episcopal jurisdiction to ecclesiastical matters, and to provide for synodical methods of episcopal government. I mean methods which will prevent autocratic action without due conference with the clergy at large and the laity.

(e) Finally, we need to remember that the governmental aspect of the episcopate, which need not and should not be autocratic, had its justification in the ancient Church not only in the tradition of its divine appointment, but in practical necessities increasingly realised in the ante-Nicene period : (a) the maintenance of unity as against Gnostic and Montanistic sects ; (b) the guarding of validity of the Eucharist and other sacramental ministrations ; (c) the preservation of the tradition of apostolic doctrine. It was then believed, and continues in Catholic Communions to be believed, that God Himself has placed upon the episcopate primarily the duty of, and responsibility for, maintaining these things in careful accord with apostolic teachings and prescriptions. It can be seen that in Catholic judgment very much indeed depends upon maintenance of the episcopate in its ancient pre-eminence and functioning.

CHAPTER VII

THE SACRAMENTS

I. *In General*

THE subjects of sacrament and priesthood are closely connected, for it is in the administration of sacraments that the most distinctive functions of priesthood emerge, and upon the effects supposed to be accomplished by the sacraments depends in large measure our conception of priesthood. It is well to consider them in immediate succession, and to make our discussion of sacraments introductory to that of priesthood.

The differences concerning the sacraments which have to be faced in labouring for reunion are related partly to doctrine concerning them and partly to their enumeration. I am not under the delusion that I can do much, if anything, for their removal. My task is to point out what seem to me to be the real issues involved, and to renew my appeal to Protestants to cease harking back to the really out-of-date forms of sixteenth-century controversies concerning them—to study them in their ecumenically established use and meaning, remembering in particular that behind ' Romish ' accretions lies an ancient consensus having antecedent traces in the New Testament itself.

In the judgment of the whole Catholic world a sacrament means an outward sign of divine appointment which when validly performed—performed according to the prescribed manner—is supernaturally efficacious, is causative of grace. This does not mean that sacramental benefits are independent of faith and penitence in the recipient. Nowhere is that believed. But it is held that the sacraments are instruments of spiritual power, by virtue of the pledged operation of the Spirit, and in their very performance—the real meaning of *ex opere operato*. A natural analogy will illustrate this. Water is by divine creation an instrument of natural power, quite apart from the subjective conditions of our drinking—i.e. *ex opere operato*, in the fact of drinking at all. But whether the drinking is beneficial or not depends upon ourselves. Under some conditions it may throw us into convulsions. The sacraments, then, as such, are instruments of spiritual power by virtue of Him who instituted them and works in them ; but they are not magical, for we cannot compel God. We cannot use them for our benefit unless we fulfil in ourselves the moral conditions under which God wills to bless us. If we use them otherwise, they remain instruments of power still, but to our spiritual damage. No doubt the theological exposition of sacraments will always vary, and within limits differences of *theological opinion* will be allowed by the Church. But what I have imperfectly set forth in this paragraph certainly describes a minimum of *doctrine* which the Catholic world does not consider open to compromise.

For several reasons, including absence of controversy requiring definition of terms, the term ' sacrament ' was variously used and applied in the patristic period. Not until scholastic theology undertook to define and co-ordinate did the term obtain the generally accepted definition made by Peter Lombard, as a divinely appointed sign and cause of sanctifying grace. Only when such definition had been fixed, could sacraments be distinguished and enumerated with finality for Catholic theologians. Henceforth the proposition that there are seven sacraments and seven only, viz., Baptism, Holy Eucharist, Confirmation, Penance, Holy Order, Matrimony, and Unction of the Sick, was accepted generally—

even in the Eastern Orthodox Churches when published there, a significant fact in view of the schism between East and West.

It can be said with some plausibility that a theological proposition which was reached only in the twelfth century cannot rank with necessary doctrines; and, subject to a rather vital proviso, I must agree. When once formulated and accepted with Catholic consent, the use of the proposition in question became the conventional method of affirming the Catholic doctrine as to each of the enumerated ' sacraments,' that it is a divinely appointed sign and cause of sanctifying grace. The proviso, then, is that a rejection of the proposition, purely theological in origin though it be, is inevitably understood as meaning a denial as to one or more of the so-called seven ' sacraments ' that it is a divinely appointed means of sanctifying grace. The Anglican formularies do not reject the septenary proposition, although they single out ' two only as generally necessary for salvation ' (in this not deviating from Catholic consent), and sharpen the distinction still further in the Articles of Religion. The Prayer Book provides for the administration of all seven except Unction of the Sick, and does not forbid its use. In America its use is now provided for. Moreover, the forms provided all plainly imply the bestowal of sanctifying grace. When the Christian world is ready for reunion, sacramental questions will no doubt have been considerably threshed out between Catholics and Protestants; and it is quite possible that the terms of reunion will not include formal acceptance of ' seven sacraments.' The fact remains that that phrase synthesises and symbolises a number of doctrines concerning the means of grace which belong to primitive tradition, and the formal denial of which the Catholic Church is not likely to permit, even for the sake of unity. These doctrines call for fresh and patient study by Protestants. I believe that some day their desire for full Christian reunion will move them to such study.

II. *Severally Considered*

It has been said that, while the sacraments must be accepted in the reunited Church, this does not hold as to theology concerning them. Like many antitheses, while punctuating a truth, the truth that what is purely theological lies beyond the range of things which can rightly be imposed as conditions of reunion, it none the less conveys to the unthinking a serious error. The error is that sacraments can be accepted either for wholesome reunion or for spiritual advantage regardless of beliefs or doctrines concerning them. Along with each sacrament goes a certain amount of doctrine as to its divine appointment, its proper minister, matter and form, and its spiritual effect. The ecclesiastically prescribed explicit form of acceptance of such doctrine has never been analytical or detailed, and is not likely to become so in the reunited Church ; but explicit rejection of a primary Catholic doctrine concerning any of the Church's sacraments will necessarily raise a barrier to reunion—more or less insurmountable according to its centrality. I now proceed to indicate as well as I can in brief synopsis the doctrine, as distinguished from theology, of each sacrament, handed down from ancient days and still maintained as of apostolic origin in the Catholic Churches. I omit provincial accretions, whether Roman or other.

(a) *Baptism* has been required as of general necessity. In extremity anyone can administer it, but the proper minister is a priest. Water must be used and applied at least to the head, the East requiring immersion. The initial effect of Baptism is an incorporation into the Body of Christ, the Church, by virtue of which the quickening life of Christ's Body is imparted and regeneration ensues. In Catholic use, regeneration does not mean conversion, but participation in the quickening vitality of Christ's Body, a fact to be remembered in connection with the prescribed Baptism of Infants. There follows remission of sins, and adoption into the special sonship of the new creation in Christ.

(*b*) *Confirmation* designates the apostolic rite of laying on of hands, whereby, we are told, the Holy Ghost is given, and which is reckoned in the Epistle to the Hebrews as one of the 'foundations.' Following apostolic usage, the Church places its administration in the control of bishops. In the East it is administered by priests, but with oil blessed for the purpose by the bishop. In the West such delegation has been exceptional and rare. The outward sign is the laying on of hands (or an equivalent use of unction, which in symbolism is obviously the same), accompanied by a formula which makes clear the purpose of the action. The grace of the sacrament consists of the sevenfold gifts of the Holy Spirit, a complement of baptismal new-birth and a needed equipment for every stage of Christian growth and warfare. Everywhere in the Ancient Church it was normally required before admission to Communion, as affording part of the spiritual equipment for worthy participation in so high a privilege. Exceptions should be confined to cases of inability to obtain Confirmation. They cannot, consistently with sacramental doctrine, be extended to cases of *refusal* to be confirmed. The teaching and ancient law of the undivided Catholic Church are involved. This law did not originate under modern conditions, it is true, but is necessitated by doctrine which no change of conditions can alter. It is to be remembered that while the modern Western separation of Confirmation from Baptism has led to insertion in the Confirmation ritual of a ratification of baptismal vows by the candidate, this ratification is an addition, and does not *constitute* Confirmation in its New Testament and Catholic meaning.

(*c*) *The Holy Eucharist*, like Baptism, has always universally been held to be generally necessary for Christians, and occupies the foremost rank among Christian institutions, celebrated every Lord's day at least, and constituting the central corporate function and worship of the faithful. It emerges in history as celebrated liturgically; and all Catholic liturgies, including the Anglican, have ever since retained a recognisable family resemblance. Non-liturgical celebrations, especially such as fail to embody our Lord's words of institution in prayer to God, would be regarded generally in the Catholic world as invalid.

The purpose of the sacrament given direct expression by Christ, and therefore primary, is that it should be done in memory of His death, to proclaim it until He comes, as St. Paul teaches. This proclamation, according to Catholic doctrine, is Godward and sacrificial. But the sacramental or grace-bestowing aspect is most conveniently dealt with here first. The minister must be at least a priest. A bishop has a prior right to officiate. The matter used must be some form of wheaten bread and pure grape wine. Grape-juice in which fermentation has been artificially prevented is invalid. If the proper matter really cannot be had, God will no doubt mercifully accept the will for the deed, even though the Eucharist, as such, fails to be validly celebrated. The formula of consecration has varied in the Church, but requires ecclesiastically appointed embodiment of our Lord's words in prayer to God, and normally includes some form of invocation of the Holy Spirit for the consecration. I have already pointed out the universal prescription of a liturgy, the chief elements of which are very ancient. The benefits of this sacrament are believed to flow from the consecrated species, the reception of which is the means of receiving the Body and Blood of Christ. From this great gift, rightly received, is derived spiritual nourishment of the soul through renewal of union with Christ.

The premise of this view of the benefit is the doctrine, most tenaciously held by the Catholic world, that the consecrated species, by virtue of Christ's own word and the operation of His Spirit, are truly although mysteriously

Christ's Body and Blood. It follows that a supernatural *change* has occurred, and that Christ is peculiarly
and objectively *present* in the sacrament. The Roman
Church, on the basis of scholastic distinctions of doubtful
validity, adds that the manner of this change is by
transubstantiation. But such doctrine has no ecumenical
authority, and the really ecumenical belief that the consecrated species have become and are the Body and Blood
of Christ ought not to be confused therewith. It should
be added that the effect of consecration was held to be as
lasting as the natural species themselves. This appears
from the very ancient general practice of reserving the
sacrament for the sick and unavoidably absent; also from
the consequent reverent care of the reserved sacrament.

That there was current in the sixteenth century a view
condemned by our Articles under the phrase ' Sacri-
fices of Masses,' according to which every Mass constitutes a fresh propitiatory sacrifice having new effects
not attributable to the sacrifice of the Cross, is true,
although not found in the best theologians of that time.
But the Catholic doctrine of Eucharistic sacrifice, than
which none is more ancient and more widely preserved,
is entirely consistent with the belief, also universally held,
that the sacrifice of the Cross is a sufficient sacrifice for
all sins, needing only to be represented, pleaded, and
applied in order to avail always and for all. But the
doctrine is that the Eucharist is the appointed means by
which Christ's members can represent and plead the
Cross before the Father and can obtain its benefits.
That the Eucharist is a derivative and applicatory
sacrifice, relative and not absolute, is a commonplace of
Catholic theology. It is called a sacrifice in that by
means of it we make the sacrifice of Christ our own in
sacramental union with Christ above.

The subject of the Holy Eucharist admits of indefinite
expansion, and much speculative theology has been
developed in relation to it. But I am here merely sum-
marising undeniable elements of ecumenical doctrine

which have to be reckoned with in promoting reunion. I wish again to remind my readers, however, that I am not trying to define the future formal terms of reunion. The effects of previous fresh study may cause them to be comparatively simple. I am merely giving a sketch of principles which the Catholic world cannot be expected to leave open to repudiation in the reunited Church. This being the case, these principles *need definition, followed by patient study*.

(*d*) *Penance* denotes the method by which the Church fulfils Christ's commission to remit sins in His name, post-baptismal sins. Its manner and conditions, obviously left to ecclesiastical ordering, underwent some development before becoming fixed early in the Middle Ages. The rule of annual confessions at Easter finally became established both East and West, but the Anglican Communion prescribes it only when the penitent is unable to quiet his conscience by other means (by *adequate* private repentance, of course). Experience has satisfied many of the high disciplinary value of more frequent use of this sacrament, and has convinced them that going to Confession is often a needed means of making repentance sufficiently complete. It is not unusual to read utterances of Protestant preachers who lament that there is not some such institution as Confession available for their use.

That Penance can be resorted to in a purely mechanical way, and that priests can be guilty of tampering with the personal integrity of penitents and spiritually enslaving them, is of course true ; but that such abuses are to-day general is a slanderous misrepresentation. I speak from some knowledge in saying so. And it is agreed among Catholic writers that an impenitent resort to Penance can result only in spiritual damage ; but, on the other hand, Penance is found to be not only an authorised means of absolution, but a means of grace both for perfecting penitence (often not otherwise adequate) and for assisting the penitent in relation to his besetting sins. Two widespread mistakes need correction : (i) it is *not* required for a good confession that every sin of whatever grade should be enumerated, but only that there should be sincere self-portrayal in relation to the forms of sin, especially graver ones, that can be recalled ; (ii) the penance imposed, technically called ' satisfaction,' is not designed as an equivalent for sin or as a price of forgiveness, but as a method by which the penitent identifies himself with Christ in His passion and *therefrom* derives help for the future. It is to avoid the very mistake referred to that penances are usually light, designed to deepen contrite resolution rather than to impart sense of achievement and of merit.

(e) *Holy Order*, or Ordination, as already sufficiently indicated, is of three grades—diaconate, priesthood, and episcopate—and its administration is reserved to bishops. In consecrating a bishop three bishops are required— not for validity, but for security of succession and to promote unity. In the ordination of priests, priests unite with the bishop in the laying on of hands. The formula accompanying the laying on of hands varies, but everywhere in the Catholic Churches the service at large makes clear both the grade to which the candidate is elevated and the sacramental grace believed to be bestowed. A typical illustration is seen in the Anglican formula for priesthood : ' Receive the Holy Ghost for the Office and Work of a Priest in the Church of God, now committed unto thee by the Imposition of our hands. Whose sins thou dost forgive, they are forgiven ; and whose sins thou dost retain, they are retained. And be thou a faithful Dispenser of the Word of God, and of His Holy Sacraments ; In the Name of the Father,' etc. This formula clearly implies that grace is being given by means of the outward sign, that is, that a sacrament is being administered.

(f) *Holy Matrimony* is a sacrament consisting of lawful marriage between baptised Christians. Unlike the other sacraments the parties to marriage are the ministers of the sacrament, although pertinent laws must be observed, and its solemnisation by a priest *ought* to be obtained. Another difference lies in the fact that not only does the marriage ceremony vary widely in different lands, but if either party is unbaptised the marriage does not become sacramental until both parties are baptised.   None the less, the sign is determinate, consisting of lawful marriage and the baptism (whether previously or later) of both parties.   When these conditions are fulfilled the sacramental conditions of divine grace for sanctification of the union to religious ends are completed, although as in all sacraments the benefits depend upon moral conditions.

In spite of practical abuses which have emerged from time to time, the Catholic doctrine is that a valid sacramental marriage cannot be reversed except by death. It is not a human contract, subject to reversal by the contracting parties.   Rather it is the *fulfilment* of a previous contract by a union having no termination except death.   It is in this, as in other regards, a type of the union between Christ and His Church.   And it is not only for the propagation of the species, but for bringing up subjects of grace in the Church of God. On no subject ought the reunited Church to give a clearer witness to the world than on this.

(g) *Unction of the Sick* is called Extreme Unction in the Roman Church, and in that Church has come to be used normally as a means of fortifying the soul *in extremis*. It is acknowledged by Roman writers, however, that this sacrament has physical recovery as a 'conditional' effect, and such recovery is the purpose for which anointing is prescribed in the New Testament.   The ancient Church inevitably treated the rite as a means of grace, because unable to dissociate *divine* healing from spiritual effects.   Being a private office, Unction does not gain mention in the sub-apostolic period, but emerges in the Nicene Age as a generally acknowledged means of healing and grace.   This status it has retained both East and West to the present time.   The first Prayer Book of Edward VI provided for it, but this provision ceased

when the second book was promulgated. The rite
has not been prohibited, however, its use is being
increasingly revived, and is officially provided for in
the revised American Prayer Book. Many feel that its
neglect among ourselves, and its normal relegation to
the moment of death in the Roman Church, have helped
to subject many for whose benefit Unction was instituted to the influence of irregular healing cults. However,
it is certain, in spite of these neglects, that the Catholic
world would refuse absolutely to permit a repudiation
of the divine appointment and sacramental nature of
Unction.

To Protestant readers much of what has been
summarised in this chapter is likely to appear remote and
impossible to accept. That this is so is evidence of the
truth of my repeated contention that fresh and prolonged
study in a new temper is the necessary antecedent of
reunion between Protestants and Catholics. What I
have here summarised ought not to be taken as the
expression of the writer's personal views merely, nor
even as distinctively Anglo-Catholic. It is an effort to
summarise elements of sacramental doctrine which *the
whole Catholic world retains as integral to the Christian
system*. I make no claim of absolute accuracy in every
detail of my statements ; but that the ecumenical position
is *substantially* such as I have described, I feel abundantly
justified in asserting. And it is surely a vain thought
that the oneness of the Christian flock can be successfully
promoted without patiently and carefully reckoning with
what seven-tenths of Christendom still considers to have
been permanently instituted for the Church by Christ,
either directly or through His Holy Spirit.

CHAPTER VIII

THE PRIESTHOOD

'WE can come to no terms with sacerdotalism,' summarises a frequent attitude of Protestants when asked to reckon with priesthood in considering the problem of reunion. The answer is twofold. In the first place the sacerdotalism thus repudiated is the corrupted form of priesthood which was revolted from in the sixteenth century. Whereas the priesthood which has to be reckoned with in promoting reunion is a reformed priesthood, not open to the objections lying behind the sweeping rejection of 'sacerdotalism.' It should be added that the evils thus stigmatised are widely abated to-day, and even in the Roman Communion are in the process of practical reformation. It is one of the conditions of reunion, reasonably certain of ultimate fulfilment, that the priesthood of the reunited Church will be free from the corruptions of the sixteenth century.

In the second place priesthood *in se*, has always been regarded as of divine appointment in the Church, was generally so regarded for many centuries, and is still retained with the same belief by a vast majority of Christians. It seems perfectly clear, therefore, that the reunion of Christendom cannot be had until the question of priesthood is frankly and patiently faced and studied, and a common solution reached that is generally perceived to be in accord with Christ's will. It is obvious that the priestly and anti-priestly standpoints carry with them mutual incongruities of practice that preclude development of the interior communion and fellowship which the Lord wills to be enjoyed by all in His Church. The question of priesthood, therefore, cannot be permanently evaded by sincere promoters of Christian reunion; and it cannot be faced rightly except in a peace-loving temper on both sides.

I. *Anglican Doctrine Catholic*

The Catholic doctrine of priesthood can be illustrated by the Anglican working system, as embodied in the Prayer Book. And this is sufficiently definitive concerning relevant doctrine and practice. But it leaves room for considerable diversity of emphasis upon its several elements, and for a wide variety of opinion concerning many theological questions. Diverse opinions gain utterance, of course, and it is important to note that the more startling, and unrepresentative of general sentiment among Anglicans they are, the more likely they are to gain public attention and be taken note of by non-Anglicans. What I am leading up to is that the real Anglican mind is not to be discovered in the utterances that are apt to be regarded as representative by outsiders. Back of these exploitings is a solid unity of mind within the Church which needs more searching inquiry to ascertain. And the official teaching of the Prayer Book retains its hold on the bulk of Anglicans amid all the disturbances of passing movements and demonstrations.

In the matter of priesthood, for example, amid differences of accent, ' high,' ' low ' and ' broad ' churchmen alike conform to a working system in which priesthood is an integral element. Their divergence, if a few unrepresentative extremists in each group are eliminated, is confined to the choice of different aspects of the priesthood for more or less exclusive emphasis. High churchmen, with varying degree of stress, emphasise the identity of the priestly order with that which existed in the Catholic Church prior to the reformation, and the supernatural and corporate aspects of its functioning. Low or Evangelical churchmen emphasise the priesthood of the laity and freedom of personal access to God. Broad churchmen emphasise the adaptation of the priesthood to modern conditions and emancipation from what they deem to be outworn shibboleths. But the united and willing adherence of all these types of churchmen to one working system and their common use of the ministry of ' priests ' prevent their divergence from having the destructive significance which it otherwise might have.

The official mind of the Anglican Communion is expressed in the Book of Common Prayer, either by direct definition and prescription or by indirect implication in what is therein required to be said and done in public worship and other official ministrations. It is pretty generally recognised among us that *lex orandi lex credendi*, the law of worship is the law of belief. That is, prescribed forms and terms in worship imply that our faith should be in harmony with the use of such forms and terms. The regular use of the Prayer Book by our people, both clerical and lay, gives its teaching a vital influence, which is often wanting to confessional documents not so repeatedly and effectively brought to the attention of the faithful.

What, then, does the Prayer Book say and require with regard to priesthood? In the first place every minister who is advanced beyond the grade of deacon is ostensibly ordained a ' priest,' the formula being, ' Receive the Holy Ghost for the Office and Work of a Priest in the Church of God, now committed unto thee by the imposition of our hands,' etc.

Moreover, the name ' priest ' is obviously used in the Prayer Book at large in a sacerdotal sense. Thus, whenever something is ordered to be said or done which pre-reformation usage restricted to *sacerdotes*, such as pronouncing absolution and celebrating the Holy

Communion or Liturgy, the officiant is designated 'priest,' whereas in all non-sacerdotal functions, such as deacons can perform, he is called 'minister.' In the American Episcopal 'Office of Institution of Ministers into Parishes or Churches' the instituted 'Presbyter' is declared to be 'possessed of full power to perform every Act of Sacerdotal Function' in the parish. The meaning of 'sacerdotal' functions is nowhere formally defined, but is to be inferred from the things which the Prayer Book requires to be done by a 'priest.' As has already been indicated, these are chiefly celebrating the liturgy and pronouncing absolution. The bishop can always act, of course, for he does not lose his priesthood through episcopal consecration. In ordaining priests the bishop says to the ordained, according to the first of two alternative forms, 'Whose sins thou dost forgive, they are forgiven; and whose sins thou dost retain, they are retained.' In the form of absolution contained in 'Order for Daily Morning Prayer' and in that for 'Daily Evening Prayer,' it is affirmed that God 'hath given power and commandment to his Ministers to declare and pronounce to his people, being penitent, the Absolution and Remission of their sins.' In the English Order for Visitation of the Sick, the priest is authorised to move the sick person to special confession, and to absolve him with use of the traditional form of the Western Church.

The importance of preserving the Order of priests from alteration is borne witness to in the Preface of the Ordinal. Here, after asserting that the ministry of bishops, priests, and deacons has existed in Christ's Church 'from the Apostles' time,' the Church says, 'And therefore to the intent that these Orders may be continued, and reverently used and esteemed in this Church, no man shall be accounted or taken to be a lawful Bishop, Priest, or Deacon, in this Church, or suffered to execute any of the said Functions except he be . . . admitted thereunto, according to the Form hereafter following, or hath had Episcopal Consecration or Ordination.' The doctrine that the Orders of the Ministry are of divine appointment emerges in the opening clause of the collect appointed to be used in ordering priests, ' Almighty God, . . . Who by Thy Holy Spirit hast appointed divers Orders of Ministers in the Church.'

To recapitulate, this Church teaches officially that that Order of priests which has existed in the Church from ancient days should be preserved as a sacred trust received from Christ and His apostles, and that none should be admitted to it except by episcopal ordination. The functions of this priesthood are delimited from those of the diaconate on the same general lines as were observed in the ancient and mediæval Church. They are made in practice chiefly to include pronouncing absolution and celebrating the Holy Communion.

II. *Theological Exposition*

My readers can perceive that, if my quotations from the Prayer Book are properly selected, they plainly teach some sort of priesthood, but not in terms which are sufficiently exclusive as to shut out a certain amount of variation in their theological interpretation—variation which has already been described in general terms, and which in Low-church circles takes the form of repudiation of ' sacerdotalism,' although accompanied by loyal conformity to a system which involves use of an Order of ' priests.' It is by Anglo-Catholics that the doctrine of priesthood is given full theological treatment, and it is this theology which I shall now summarise.

To begin with, they accept the *positives* on this subject of Low and Broad churchmen. With the former they believe in lay priesthood, and with the latter they recognise the necessity of adapting priesthood to the conditions of each successive age. Their characteristic emphasis, however, is placed upon the distinctive

G

functions of priesthood, upon the official and corporate aspects of ministerial as distinguished from lay priesthood. Making much of the Catholic inheritance of the Anglican Communion, they believe that the Anglican Church intends no other changes from pre-reformation principles than it explicitly sets forth in the Prayer Book. In brief, they hold that the Church intends no breach of continuity with the past, but retains as a matter of course every integral element of ancient Catholic doctrine and practice. Accordingly, they interpret the Prayer Book language concerning priesthood as substantially identical in meaning with the Catholic doctrine of antiquity. And they consider this interpretation to be supported by sufficient evidence contained in official documents of the Anglican reformation.

(a) From this standpoint they maintain that Christ gave to the Church a share on earth not only in His prophetic and kingly office but also in His priesthood. He gave this to the whole Church, and every baptised member of the Church inherits a share in the gift. The laity then as truly have part in the ' royal priesthood ' of which St. Peter speaks as do official ministers.

(b) But they hold that this priesthood is corporate. It was not bestowed upon a mere collection of individual believers, but upon a society then being organised around the apostolic nucleus. This society was not, properly speaking, a volunteer association, but the Lord's own creation. It was to be endowed with the Holy Spirit, and thus to be brought into those vital, corporate, and structural relations to its Creator which we symbolise when, after the example of St. Paul, we call the Church the Body of Christ. Whatever we are in Christ we are as in His mystical Body, the Church—the relation being social, corporate, and subject to organic differentiation. All the members of the Body share in its priestly functioning, but each member in a manner determined by his place in the Body. ' Not all have the same office ' in the common priesthood.

(*c*) The difference between lay priesthood and that of priests in the more technical sense, is between ministerial or official, and unofficial. A ministerial priest acts representatively for the whole mystical Body of Christ—not as a substitute, nor externally, but as an organ in corporate functioning of the whole Church. The priest is one of the faithful, distinguishable from the rest only by organic relations in the common functioning of the Body. He acts among, as well as for, the rest. They 'assist' and use him, because along with him they constitute the Body which functions corporately by his ministry. Therefore he does not come between them and God, whether we consider them collectively or as individuals. All act together in matters of corporate functioning, although each acts in his own way according to his place in the whole mystical Body.

(*d*) The functions ascribed to priesthood are twofold, having to do with the bestowal of gifts from God to the members of Christ's Body and with their corporate approach to God. I have described these functions as corporate. The members of Christ are members one of another, even in their deepest relations to God. These relations are not exclusively corporate, and what is called 'personal religion' is a very real and precious thing. But the personal is dependent upon the social and corporate. We are by nature social and mutually dependent beings. So it is that, in our conception of things, God wills to bestow His grace in and through Christ, but through Him as Head of a mystical Body, the members of which are to be nourished and blessed in their corporate relationship.

This determines the external organisation of the Church, through which the manner of Christ's mediation is visibly corporate and ministerial. And this corporate method holds in our approach to the Father; and our mutual relations in the Body of Christ control the manner in which we employ His mediation, a manner necessarily ministerial.

Our liturgy embodies both of these aspects of priesthood. In it, on the one hand, the Church lays hold upon the spiritual nourishment of Christ's Body and Blood, received from Him, and distributes the gift through its ministers to the faithful. In it also, on the other hand, she makes a solemn approach to God, with a memorial of Christ's death—an oblation in which all identify themselves with the great sacrifice of Calvary and plead its merits. It is a corporate action; and is, therefore, fulfilled liturgically, and in a manner believed to have been appointed by Christ Himself.

(e) The earthly priest is a minister of Christ, serving in His priesthood, and employed by Him in condescension to those human limitations which our natural and social dependence upon each other's ministry imposes. We believe that we can gain effective help, and can adequately express our relations to God in worship, only in a manner agreeing with our mutual dependence in every ramification of receptivity and expression.

(f) We hold that the manner of priestly functioning is determined—not by human arrangements, nor on lines that can be essentially changed, but—by the structural nature of the Body of Christ, which comes from Him. No other body on earth can function in priesthood except the Body of Christ, and it can function only through the organism and ministry which Christ has given to it. Speaking in historical terms, this means to us that the ministerial structure of Christ's Body on earth is represented by the three sacred Orders of bishops, priests, and deacons, as perpetuated by an unbroken continuity of episcopal consecration or ordination. This is not belief in a caste, but in an organism. The priesthood draws its members from the faithful at large, regardless of any undemocratic distinctions. The family affords a partial analogy. It also is of divine ordering and organic. To call it undemocratic is to use a non-relevant description, and to us it is no more difficult to reconcile a sacerdotal ministry with democratic ideals than it is to do the same for the sacred institution of parents. We conceive both institutions to be divine and both to leave the equality of souls before God entirely unaffected.

III. *Objections*

I understand the more acute Protestant objections to ministerial priesthood to be two : (*a*) that priests come between souls and God, invading the sole mediatorship of Christ, and hampering freedom of access to God ; (*b*) that the New Testament affords no warrant for such priesthood. The limited purpose of this book precludes my dealing with these objections except in an incipient way, that is, by indicating summarily the considerations which in Catholic judgment meet these objections.

(*a*) The first objection concerns two alleged consequences of ministerial priesthood : interference with the freedom of souls in access to God, and invasion of Christ's sole mediatorship.

(i) Postponing the question of mediatorship for the moment, it has to be admitted that if the ministerial priesthood is either of human invention or corruptly and tyrannically exercised, it is certain to upset the spiritual liberties of individual souls and to hamper their freedom of access to God. If, however, it is not of human invention, but of divine appointment, as Catholics believe, then it cannot *as such* be prejudicial to access to God. The question of divine appointment will be considered soon. The Catholic contention is that the hampering effects of priesthood or personal religion have been due to its corrupt exercise, and are removable by reformation. And such reformation, as distinguished from rejection, has in fact been going on apace, and the situation in Catholic Churches to-day, generally speaking, is much improved over that of the sixteenth century.

The practice of personal religion, or the cultivation by believers of individual and private relations with God, prevails within Catholic as well as Protestant Churches.

The lives of Catholic saints illustrate this. But there is a difference. A Protestant feels that his personal access to God requires protection from the encroachments of corporate religion, in particular of ministerial priesthood. A Catholic, on the other hand, combines the corporate and personal without fear. He discovers in corporate religion, sacramental and sacerdotal, a source of security and enrichment for his personal religion and a safeguard against individualism and spiritual anarchy. He believes that, inasmuch as his relation to God is both individual and corporate, both must be provided for, and neither one can be rightly developed in isolation from the other.

Grave as the consequences of corruption of the priesthood have been, they may easily be exaggerated. Much depends upon whether individuals believe in priesthood as of divine appointment. Such believers will mourn the presence of priestly corruption; but, in spite of that corruption, they will find the appointed sacramental ministrations of their priests a source of grace which supports their personal religion instead of hampering it. In the darkest period of mediæval corruption the Church was developing many souls in holiness, often in conspicuous degree.

(ii) The sole mediatorship of Christ is not less a truism in Catholic than in Protestant theology. But Catholic theology applies the principle comprehensively to our Lord's prophetic and kingly as well as to His priestly office. And this explains the Catholic insistence that no earthly ministry should be recognised in the Church unless it can be shown to have been appointed by Christ. The doctrine of apostolic succession is thus ancillary to the doctrine of Christ's sole mediatorship. The question, in particular, whether ministerial priesthood is an invasion of this mediatorship depends for answer upon the question whether Christ instituted such priesthood. If He did, the Christian priest is Christ's minister, and His ministrations constitute a method by which the sole Mediator exercises His office on earth. We come, then, to the second objection, that the New Testament affords no warrant for such priesthood.

(b) It is to be acknowledged that the title priest is nowhere given to a Christian minister in the New Testament. In view of the fact that many Jewish priests were obedient to the faith such usage would have been confusing, to say the least. The question then is, Were Christian ministers exercising priestly functions? In so far as they administered the sacraments, and employed the power of forgiving and retaining sins, they did exercise them; and St. Paul describes himself as doing so in Romans xv, 16. This appears more clearly in the original Greek than in the English.

Priesthood comes to the fore in sacrifice, and Christian priesthood notably declares itself in the Eucharistic sacrifice. The term sacrifice is nowhere definitely applied to the Eucharist in the New Testament. The reason seems clear. The believers in Jerusalem continued to frequent the sacrificial worship of the Temple, and to designate the Eucharist as a sacrifice would have bred confusion and controversy. The difficulty was parallel to that of calling Christian ministers priests. None the less, the Eucharist is described in terms that justify calling it a sacrifice, in particular in 1 Cor. x, 16–21 and in the accounts of the institution. It is significant that the destruction of Jerusalem, which terminated the necessity among Christians of reckoning with Jewish priesthood and sacrifice, was quickly followed by the development of unmistakably sacrificial and sacerdotal description of the Eucharist and its ministers. I am merely indicating data with which to reckon in studying this subject, and cannot take space to elaborate the argument.

The formal argument for priesthood in the Church is of course an appeal to the Lord's commission. Whether the Fourth Gospel gives the precise language of Christ or not, the words ' As My Father hath sent Me, even so send I you,' appear to be borne out by all relevant expressions attributed to Him in the other Gospels. The meaning at large appears to be that Christ commissioned His ministers to continue His own earthly ministry, as His agents, of course. No exceptions emerge. He was prophet, priest, and king, and they were to minister in His Name in all these directions—teaching, ministering the sacraments of grace and worship, and exercising the disciplinary cure of souls. And if the prophetic and kingly (pastoral) aspects of the Christian ministry do not constitute invasion of the Lord's sole mediatorship, it is difficult to explain why the priestly aspect does this. The reason why they do not is the same in each case. It lies in the Lord's commission, and in the fact that in every function the Christian minister is merely minister. All that He does has its effect in the pledged action of Christ through His Holy Spirit. Abuses may indeed shorten the benefits of priesthood to many souls, but they cannot nullify it so as to deprive *faithful* souls of what it has been appointed to convey.

CHAPTER IX

VALIDITY

THE aim of this chapter is to deal more fully than I have thus far done with the contentious term 'validity.' There has been no official Anglican pronouncement declaring non-episcopal ministries to be invalid, but the Preface of the Anglican Ordinal has been taken to declare episcopal ordination to be necessary for validity, although such form of expression is not used in it. Unquestionably Catholic believers, whether Anglican or other, do hold non-episcopal ministries to be invalid. On the other hand, Anglican Catholics have repeatedly acknowledged the fact, established by abundant evidence, that God has blessed the ministrations of non-episcopal ministers. Protestants have taken such acknowledgments as inconsistent with the opinion that non-episcopal ministries are invalid; and ask in effect, If our ministry is blessed of God, why do you not recognise it as a valid ministry of Christ's Universal Church? In the conferences between the Lambeth Committee and the Free Churches' Committee, the Anglican participants expressed the view that the terms 'valid' and 'invalid' ought to be abandoned. And they declared non-episcopal ministries to be 'real ministries . . . in the Universal Church,' language subsequently qualified by the denial that they have the authority of the Universal Church.

Such language, due undoubtedly to a desire to be as eirenic as possible, had the effect of clouding rather than

clearing the subject. The phrase ' real ministries '
suggests, without necessarily meaning, ' valid
ministries '; and a retention and correct definition of the
term ' valid ' is essential to a clear exposition of the
Catholic view of non-episcopal ministries. This view is
entirely consistent with belief that God has blessed non-
episcopal ministrations, but precludes their acknowledgment as ' valid ' ministries *of* the Universal Church.

The word ' valid ' has various meanings, according to
the connection in which it is used. In law, for example,
a valid marriage means one that has been lawfully performed. Some of our writers have taken over this
meaning into sacramental use, and have said that a valid
sacrament or ministry means one that conforms to the
canon law of the Church; and they have explained that
to call a non-episcopal ministry invalid means simply
that it does not accord with canon law, and has not the
authority of the Catholic Church. Many at least of
Protestant leaders would acknowledge so much; but
might ask, In the interests of unity, and for avoidance of
slur on past Protestant ministrations confessedly blessed
of God, why cannot the Anglican Communion give
formal recognition to non-episcopal ministers and thus
remove their canonical irregularity? The answer is
twofold. Such recognition would be purely provincial,
would add another obstacle to reunion between the
Anglicans and the rest of the Catholic world; and, if
uncoupled with episcopal ordination, would not repair
the lack of validity in the traditional Catholic use of that
term.

The point is that in Catholic use ' valid,' while normally
presupposing ' canonical ' or ' regular,' means more. *It
means that the sacrament or ministry concerned has been performed or conferred in conformity with the primitive arrangements
of Christ and His Spirit for the Church.* To the Church,
according to Catholic belief, pertains the authority to
define what such conformity requires. But even the
Universal Church cannot deviate from the original divine

arrangements. It cannot truly declare valid any sacrament or ministry in which the conformity mentioned is lacking.

The real issue, then, is clear. When Catholics deny the validity of non-episcopal ministries or sacraments they mean simply that they do not conform in all essentials to the arrangements of Christ and His Holy Spirit for the Church, and that apart from episcopal ordination in line with ' apostolic succession ' such ministries cannot be made valid. Mere recognition would leave this essential of validity unsupplied. Protestants, on the other hand, deny that episcopacy, and what is called ' apostolic succession ' by means of episcopacy, are of divine appointment. They also appeal to the evidences of divine blessing upon their ministry, evidences frankly acknowledged by many Catholics, as calling for its recognition as from God.

The Catholic answer to this Protestant appeal to spiritual fruits is based upon the premise that, although the Church is bound by divine arrangements, and no one may count on divine blessing if he knowingly and avoidably fails to conform to them, God's mercy is not bound by them in relation to those who, from whatever just cause, mistake their requirements, while sincerely seeking to fulfil the will of Christ. It is not directly relevant, but most of us, I think, believe that God's blessing, in lesser degree no doubt, extends to multitudes of earnest seekers after God who have no knowledge of Christ and His divine claim. The Protestant revolt was due to acute provocation, to abuses which obscured the claim of the episcopate. Their rejection of it was not wittingly a rejection of divine arrangements for the Church, and those who inherit the four-century Protestant tradition are surely not guilty of conscious departure from these arrangements. As sincere disciples of Christ, conforming to His will as they believe it to be, God blesses them abundantly.

The fact remains that they are out of communion with

the Catholic hierarchy and, according to Catholic belief, have in important ways departed from the arrangements of Christ for His Church. That such departure involves *no* spiritual loss is a very precarious proposition indeed. In the reunited Church these arrangements must be safeguarded, and the larger part of Christendom holds that this cannot be done unless all the Church's ministers are episcopally ordained.

Such is the issue. I am not under the delusion that my statement of it will convince Protestants forthwith. My aim is more modest—to do what I can toward clearing the way for a fresh study of the questions which now divide Christians. Protestants are not asked to accept what they designate as ' prelacy ' and ' sacerdotalism.' But they ought to study episcopacy and priesthood in their purity, undistracted by memories of the sixteenth century. History does not repeat itself.

I conclude this chapter with one more matter. The members of non-episcopal ministries refuse to submit to episcopal ordination on the ground that they will thereby imply that they have not already been ordained and will repudiate a ministry which has been manifestly blessed of God. From the Catholic standpoint, as explained above, neither consequence will be involved. To submit to ordination to the appointed ministry of the Universal Church would be to acknowledge *first*, that although for special reasons God has used and blessed a non-episcopal ministry, it is not the ministry appointed of God for the Church Universal, and *secondly* that the call to reunion is to be answered by all once more rallying to the support of the ministry which is thus appointed. The previous non-episcopal ministry, in other words, may be regarded as an emergency provision to meet sixteenth-century abuses, a provision which has fulfilled its purpose and which should therefore give way to the ancient ministry of the Universal Church. I admit that Protestants are not yet ready to consider their ministry in this light, but this is a branch of the difficulty that true reunion—the reunion of Christendom—is not yet in sight. Much fresh study is needed.

It is assumed, and the assumption is general in the Catholic world, that whatever may be acknowledged as to the spiritual fruit of non-episcopal ministries, they are *other* ministries than that of the Church Universal. And this view seems to be supported by the Protestant repudiation of ministerial priesthood. A ministry which disclaims sacerdotal functioning can hardly be the same with that which makes such functioning central. When a deacon is ordained to the priesthood, it is not called reordination, as if his previous ministry, within its limits, were unfruitful. What happens is the deacons' ordination to a *new* office, confessedly not possessed previously, the sacerdotal office.

If Protestants come to accept the Catholic doctrine of ministerial priesthood, they will look on submission to episcopal ordination in an analogous light—not as a reflection on the past but as ordination to a priesthood not previously theirs, themselves being witness. I do not forget that Protestants now deny the sacerdotal claim of the Catholic ministry. But I am indicating the ecumenical or Catholic point of view. And Protestants ought not to resent an effort to present that standpoint frankly when the reunion of Christendom is at stake. And it is part of my purpose in laying Catholic cards on the table not only to appeal for fresh study, but also to make clear the present futility of schematic action for reunion between Catholic (including Anglican) and Protestant Churches. Friendly co-operation on lines involving no compromise or appearance of it, and in devout study of the questions of Faith and Order involved, is the only available line of progress at this stage.

CHAPTER X

I. *Lausanne Statements of Agreement*

THE report on 'the Church's Common Confession of Faith,' received by the Lausanne Conference, says, 'Notwithstanding the differences in doctrine among us, we are united in a common Christian Faith which is proclaimed in the Holy Scriptures and is witnessed to and safeguarded in the Ecumenical Creed, commonly called the Nicene, and in the Apostles' Creed, which Faith is continuously confirmed in the spiritual experience of the Church of Christ.' Note 2, appended to this report, reads, 'It must be noted also that some of the Churches represented in this Conference conjoin tradition with the Scriptures, some are explicit in subordinating Creeds to the Scriptures, some attach a primary importance to their particular Confessions, and some make no use of Creeds.' Note 3 says, 'It is understood that the use of these Creeds will be determined by the competent authority in each Church, and that the several Churches will continue to make use of such special Confessions as they possess.'

The Orthodox Easterns abstained from voting on this and other Reports, explaining in a formal statement that their drafting 'was carried out on the basis of compromise between what in our understanding are conflicting ideas and meanings, in order to arrive at an external agreement in the letter alone : whereas, as has oftentimes been emphasised in statement by representatives of the Orthodox Church, in matters of faith and conscience there is room for no compromise. For us, two different meanings cannot be covered by, and two different concepts cannot be deduced from, the same words of a generally agreed statement. Nor can we Orthodox hope that an agreement reached upon such statements would remain lasting.'

The Orthodox spoke truly in criticising the ambiguity of the Reports, in particular of the Report from which I have quoted ; and there were other representatives who abstained from voting, without advertising the fact. They indeed expressed the mind of every consistently Catholic representative ; and had it not been for certain weighty reasons, if I can judge from expressions conveyed to me, Anglo-Catholic representatives would also have issued a joint statement either endorsing the language of the Orthodox or expressing essentially the same position in their own way. The reasons against doing this were : (*a*) the undesirability of acting apart from other Anglican representatives ; (*b*) the fact that the Reports contained sufficient statements of differences to prevent the ambiguities in statements of agreement from being misleading ; (*c*) the insertion in the Preamble of the Reports of acknowledgment that the Reports were ' neither exhaustive nor in all details satisfactory to every member of the Conference, we submit them to the Churches for that deliberate consideration which could not be given in the brief period of our sessions ' ; (*d*) the rule of the Conference that the Reports should be ' received ' rather than ' adopted.' In brief, in spite of the form of the Reports they were in effect not Reports of agreements adopted by the Conference, but Reports of incomplete discussions, received rather than adopted because not thoroughly threshed out. To vote for the reception of such Reports, under such limitations, could not commit the voter to any specific statement contained in them.

The reason why I have given this explanation is to

justify the statement which I now make that, while the will to agree was much in evidence at Lausanne, the actual amount of agreement there shown has certainly been exaggerated in some quarters. The statements of agreement voted on were in vital particulars ambiguous; and if they had stood by themselves, without the accompanying statements of differences and the limiting provisos above mentioned, they could have secured only a divided vote.

In fact, the Catholic and Protestant Churches differ both as to important contents of the Faith and as to the Rule of Faith whereby the claim of any doctrine to be *de fide* is tested. Moreover, Protestant Churches, while generally united in making Holy Scripture the sole standard and rule of the Faith, show serious mutual conflicts of doctrine in their Confessions. And there has been a formidable development of Liberalism, especially among Protestants, claiming freedom to interpret the language of Creeds and Confessions symbolically and in senses inconsistent with their original and official meaning. They definitely reject certain very central articles of the ecumenical Creeds. It is evident that the reunion of Christendom cannot be had until these differences are frankly faced and carefully studied, and until by such means, and by the guidance of the Spirit, common and sincere acceptance of the historic Christian Faith is obtained.

To call pointed attention to existing differences, and to urge their patient consideration, is not, as is sometimes said, an evidence of lack of sincere desire for reunion, but is to plead for the only possible method of bringing about true reunion—the reunion of Christendom. It may, of course, be said that the agreement of which I speak is impossible. It is so without divine aid, but such aid is assured to those who seek it; and to say that Christians can never be united in essential doctrine is equivalent to denial of the power of truth to prevail. The reason why the matter is vital is that doctrine determines life, both for individuals and in corporate practice. This can be seen in the numerous differences in religious ideals and practice between Catholics and Protestants. So it is that a union which leaves discordant doctrine unremedied also leaves practical grounds of friction in full power. It is not wholesome and cannot be permanent. But Christ wills one flock, and this requires us not only to labour for the reunion of all Christendom, but to seek that unity of faith which is essential to its achievement and wholesome permanence. It is not at all necessary for the unity of faith referred to that differences of theological opinion should disappear. What is required is that Christendom should have one mind as to what has been once for all revealed to the Church, that is, as to the certainties in the light of which we are enabled to work out our salvation and find our way home to God. The theological context of this faith always has varied and always will vary, and so long as its variations leave the Faith in effective possession and substantially unchanged they need not disturb Christian consciences.

II. *Conflicting Rules of Faith*

The doctrinal agreement of the Catholic Churches, still continuing in spite of centuries of schism and mutual antagonism, is very notable in range, and has the effect of also preserving in the worship, sacramental life, and practical discipline of these Churches an evident family likeness. The rejection by the Eastern Orthodox and Anglican Churches of Roman claims and assertions, so far from altering the impressiveness of the agreement which survives, really intensifies it.

On the other hand, the doctrinal agreement of Protestant Churches is significantly reduced, their Confessions of Faith and consequent divergent polities being witness. There is indeed a tendency to speak of an Evangelical Faith, supposed to be commonly accepted

H

by Protestants ; but no definition of it which does not admit of important divergence in its interpretation is forthcoming. That the pre-eminence of Christ is generally accepted is true, but concerning His personal claim and the Faith which He came to reveal much disagreement exists. To-day, partly because of the growth of Liberalism, and partly because of recoil from the evils of disunion, there is considerable tendency to disparage the need of doctrinal agreement—as if the reunion of Christendom could be had without it.

What is the cause of this contrast between many centuries of large Catholic consent in doctrine and the doctrinal variations of Protestantism ? It apparently lies in the divergent Rules of Faith whereby Catholics and Protestants respectively determine or test the doctrines which they accept as essentials of the Christian Faith. Following the mind of the ancient Churches, Catholics continue to accept the two-fold authority of the Church's doctrinal tradition and of Scripture, the former being treated as interpreting the latter. Protestants, on the other hand, make the Bible the sole source and standard of doctrine, and in its interpretation substitute spiritually enlightened private judgment for the Church's Spirit-guided doctrinal tradition. The Catholic Rule, the Church to teach and define and the Bible to test, confirm, and illustrate, has established a somewhat comprehensive Catholic faith which, with whatever distinctively provincial accretions, has for many centuries retained the consent of Eastern, Roman, and Anglican Churches—seven-tenths of Christendom—in spite of schism and mutual suspicion. The Protestant Rule resulted at once in eliminating significant elements of the Catholic doctrinal tradition, and set in motion the mutual doctrinal divergence to which reference has been made above.

If the reader thinks that in contrasting the working values of the Catholic and Protestant Rules of Faith I am drifting into polemics—inconsistent with my avowed aim of promoting reunion—I beg him to reckon with the purpose for which I have made the contrast. That purpose is to bring into view a chief cause of the present doctrinal differences in Christendom, which is the abandonment by Protestants of the well-tested historic Rule of Faith and the substitution therefor of a Rule which has failed to work—failed to preserve a comprehensive doctrinal consent among those who have accepted it. My argument is strictly relevant to the promotion of reunion. In brief statement it is this : The reunion of Christendom plainly depends upon a common Faith, upon agreement concerning doctrines deemed vital to true religion. Such agreement obviously cannot be had without a common Rule of Faith ; and, as between the Catholic and Protestant Rules, the Catholic Rule has preserved a large and significant agreement in doctrine, whereas the Protestant Rule has failed to do this. These facts, I argue, show that if the doctrinal unity upon which the reunion of Christendom depends is to be reached, it must be on the basis of the Rule of Faith which has worked, the Catholic Rule.

It must be confessed that in the sixteenth century the unity of doctrine in the matter of adherence to the primitive Faith still prevailing in the Church was obscured, and reduced in value for many, by the accretions and corruptions of the Western Church, and by the then tendency of ecclesiastics to treat mediæval accretions as if they were *de fide*. It was natural that many earnest souls should see no way of return to primitive purity of doctrine except the rejection of ecclesiastical tradition and the adoption of Holy Scripture as the *sole* Rule of Faith. But the Catholic Rule of Faith does not involve acceptance of mediæval or modern accretions ; for, according to its proper meaning, the Church which is to teach and define is the Catholic Church universal, not the Roman Church apart from the rest. And, according to the same rule, at least implicitly presupposed in it, what the Church is authorised to teach and define consists exclusively of the Faith once for all delivered to the saints. The Church is witness to what it has received, not a creator of substantially new doctrine. The doctrine to which its Rule points is that which has been held by the Church *everywhere* (by all parts of the Catholic Church), *always* (from the beginning), and *by all* (all representative theologians, in matters wherein they are reputed to be orthodox). Reunion depends not only upon restoration of the ancient Rule of Faith, but also upon a denial to all accretions, even to tolerable speculative opinions, of any binding authority for individual believers. Both the recovery of losses and the purging out of provincial excesses in doctrinal requirements are needed. The relative emphasis of my treatment of these two needs is due to the fact that my argument is addressed to those who accept, or are influenced by, the Protestant Rule of Faith.

III. *Working Value of the Catholic Rule*

The need of a common Rule of Faith for reunited Christendom is clearly very central. I hope to be pardoned, therefore, if I go on to explain what appear to me to be the reasons for the relative smallness and largeness of the unity of doctrine secured respectively by the Protestant and the Catholic Rule of Faith.

(*a*) Why does the Bible fail to work—fail to secure any considerable doctrinal unity—when made to serve as exclusive source and standard? The Anglican Articles of Religion, in agreement with the Catholic world, assert that all saving doctrine is *contained* in Scripture; and, inasmuch as, therefore, no doctrine can rightly be regarded as necessary which disagrees with Scripture sanely interpreted, we all admit that Scripture is the *final test* of Christian doctrine. But, whatever may be the experience of individuals here and there, the Bible was not historically the source for the Church of its Faith. The convincing proof is that the Church was

already teaching its faith before one word of the New
Testament had been written, long before the Canon of
the New Testament was available. Moreover, it may be
doubted whether any large proportion of Protestants
really derive their faith *in the first instance* from Scripture.
Usually they imbibe it from their elders, and then test
what they thus receive by the Bible—that is, if they are
thoughtful enough to do so. Moreover, even when
they do test it, their interpretation is apt to be determined practically by the exegetical tradition of their
denomination. Really independent derivation of the
individual's faith from Scripture is not common. In
other words, Protestants as well as Catholics in ordinary
practice appear to receive their faith from extra-biblical
sources before testing it by Scripture ; and in such testing
rarely exercise pure private judgment. The difference
lies in the extra-biblical source deferred to and in the fact
that, unlike Protestants, Catholics consciously recognise
this extra-biblical source as being the immediate,
authoritative, and definitive source of their Faith.

The fact is that the Bible is not suited for the use to
which Protestants would put it, being a very miscellaneous
collection of memorials of experience rather than a
definitive manual. Its meaning is often far from being
self-evident ; and, without previous indoctrination in
the religion and Faith which is usually taken for granted
rather than defined in its pages, ordinary readers are
quite unequal to deriving a consentient Faith from it by
exclusively private judgment. Even among experts the
differences in exegesis of passages of critical doctrinal
bearing are notorious. Only a common Faith *previously
accepted* enables biblical scholars to reach agreement as to
the essentials of biblical doctrine. It is the previously
accepted and common confessional standpoint which
accounts for the measures of agreement in biblical
exegesis found between scholars in each several denomination ; and it is the attempted independence of such bias,
as they call it, which explains the fragmentariness and

mutual discordances of doctrine derived from Scripture by Liberals or Modernists.

Intelligent investigation of biblical doctrine appears to be impossible without a previously adopted doctrinal standpoint, and upon the correctness of that standpoint depends the soundness of the results of such investigation. Entirely unbiased study of Scripture seems to mean empty-minded, unintelligent, study. It gets nowhere. As a final test of previously received doctrine, and as *able to make believers wise unto salvation*, the Bible has been vindicated by Christian experience. But the effort to make it the sole source and self-sufficient standard of the Faith, as interpreted by private judgment, has failed practically to preserve a common Faith among those who try thus to proceed. I say ' try,' for the procedure referred to is honoured in theory rather than in observance ; and, in general Protestant practice, the real standard of Faith is the Confession of Faith or at least the characteristic outlook of some denomination. Liberals may be excepted, but their view of biblical authority is not that presupposed in either the Protestant or the Catholic Rule of Faith. In this argument, therefore, the exception is negligible.

(*b*) The Catholic Rule of Faith avowedly prepares the members of the Church for the study of Scripture by previous instruction in the Church's traditional doctrine. It answers the question, How can I understand ' except some man should guide me ? ' (Acts viii, 31) by teaching the inquirer, through appointed ministers, the traditional Catholic Faith, as affording a general clue to the doctrinal meaning of Scripture. The Church claims the authority thus to teach and define the Faith partly upon the basis of the Lord's commission and partly because of the pledged guidance of the Spirit. This guidance was not promised to individuals in mutual isolation, but in an organic communion which led the primitive Christians to continue ' stedfastly in the Apostles' doctrine and fellowship ' (Acts ii, 42), and to cultivate the same mind and judgment (1 Cor. i, 10).

The ancient Church's response to this guidance was the adoption of manifold and mutually corroborative methods of guarding its tradition of doctrine from any essential alteration. It serves my argument to specify these methods—methods which have been continued to this day. It should be said at the outset, however, that this tradition was not derived by the Church from Scripture, although fortified by an appeal to Old Testament prophecy, but from the direct teaching of Christ and His Holy Spirit before the New Testament existed.

We should remember that this tradition was not merely a personal transmission of doctrine by word of mouth. Such transmission was indeed prominent at first ; and, so long as Christian teachers were still living who had listened to the Apostles, it was dependable. But before sufficient time had elapsed to weaken its value, it was re-enforced by several other methods of tradition.

From the start the breaking of bread or Holy Eucharist became the central corporate function of the Church, being celebrated at least every week. And it rapidly took on the form of a liturgy, in which the leading Articles of the Faith were given clear witness. Recent research has shown a striking resemblance between the various local liturgies of the post-apostolic period, a resemblance suggesting a common earlier source, presumably apostolic. Even now, the liturgies of the Catholic Churches, East and West, including the Anglican, preserve this resemblance ; and they continue uninterruptedly to reflect in their phrases those elements of the Faith which, if fully assimilated, involve acceptance of the rest. The Resurrection had from the outset the additional memorial of the weekly Lord's Day ; and the Christian Calendar, still fundamentally the same in every Catholic Church, was developed to keep in memory the more significant contents of the original Gospel.

The apostolic ' form of sound words ' gradually took the form of the various Creeds of local Churches, which received verbal amendments designed to guard against post-apostolic errors. The so-called Apostles' Creed has been traced by some as far back as the beginning of the second century. The Nicene Creed, so called, is the Creed of the Church of Jerusalem, with the Nicene phrase, ' consubstantial with the Father,' inserted, in order to shut out the Arian denial of our Lord's true Godhead.

Then there are such rites as Confirmation, Penance, Ordination, and so forth, derived from apostolic days and embodying in various ways the elements of Faith which we still find in them.

(c) It is clear that the several ancient elements of the Church's officially prescribed working system have borne abiding and mutually corroborative witness in all parts of the Catholic Church to the primitive Faith, and have done so in manners least liable either to be misunderstood or to be substantially changed. Inasmuch as their witness is official, representing continuous and accordant Catholic requirement in the long past *and to-day*, it constitutes the living voice of the Church corporate, a voice which, in spite of additions and schisms, still enforces the ancient Faith in all parts of the Catholic Church— Eastern, Roman, and Anglican. In the Anglican Prayer Book, it is sufficiently made available to all, of every grade of intelligence. This Church welcomes very free inquiry, and is very tolerant of passing vagaries ; but it shows by what it prescribes to be said and done that it stands officially for the unaltered Faith and Order of the great Catholic Church.

The Church fortifies its tradition by using Holy Scripture to test the conformity of its later teaching with that of primitive days. Historically the Scriptures are incidental products of the Church's working life. Some of them, indeed, are fruits of high degrees of prophetic inspiration ; but all presuppose the Church's existing Faith, and are designed, in language adapted to other times and conditions than ours, to make believers therein wise unto salvation.

None the less, by effective overruling of a long process of human producing, editing, redacting, selecting, and ecclesiastical canonising, the Holy Spirit has made the Bible to be the Church's divine library for the edification of the faithful.   As thus produced and given, it is called ' the Word of God.'   This does not make it the source of formal doctrinal definition.   But it *does* enable the Church's intelligent disciples to test the agreement of the Church's current doctrine with its originally received Faith.

Accordingly, as we have seen, the Catholic Rule by which to distinguish the original and unchanging Christian Faith from all else is to accept the authority which the Church has received from Christ to teach and define, and to test Church doctrine by its harmony with Scripture.   This means practically that we should bring to the test of Scripture that Faith which is defined in its leading elements in the Nicene and Apostles' Creeds and is embodied in the liturgical and sacramental offices of the Church.

Such a rule saves us from the confusion that besets those who look for guidance to original preachers and writers of the moment rather than to the Church's authoritative teaching.   It also explains the fact that, under the Spirit's promised guidance, the Catholic Churches, in spite of their quarrels and provincial accretions, still retain the whole Faith and Order of the undivided primitive Church.   And no corresponding consent appears to be elsewhere existent or attainable. Great scholars are found in both of the two chief sections of Christendom ; but not until all observe one Rule of Faith can they agree sufficiently to fulfil the Lord's will ' that they all may be one.'

IV. *Creeds and Confessions*

Two matters connected with the necessity of a common Rule of Faith in the reunited Church require brief attention in this chapter: the use of the Catholic Creeds and the continued use by the several Churches of their special Confessions.

(*a*) It is of course inevitable that the several local Churches in reunited Christendom will have their own regulations as to the use of the Catholic Creeds, and that these regulations will vary. But both the Catholic emphasis on doctrinal stewardship and the necessity which all who are ready for real unity in fundamental doctrine will feel that this unity should be adequately safeguarded will operate to impose certain limits upon such variation. In an effectively united Christendom the ecumenical mind will necessarily be dominant, and that mind is not likely to tolerate any provincial use of the ancient Creeds which will have the effect of making them remote and of reducing the general sense of responsibility for their acceptance by individual believers. No doubt the full meaning of these Creeds is not grasped by untrained believers ; but even such can reasonably be asked, in the interests of doctrinal unity, to accept ' sound words ' which for many centuries have been the normal and authoritative expression of such unity in the universal Church.

Pleas were made at Lausanne for freedom in the interpretation of these Creeds. The word interpretation has two distinct uses, although those who thus plead usually do not distinguish them. According to one use, to interpret a Creed means to exhibit the relations and bearings of the doctrines which it affirms, whether in relation to systematic theology, to modern knowledge and thought, or to moral and spiritual applications. In this sense Creed-interpretation cannot be shackled without disastrous obscurantism resulting. The Creeds are not imposed as *boundaries* of Christian thought and opinion but as sound, safeguarding, and enlightening *premises* thereof. It is absurd to expect that freedom of interpretation in this sense will be lacking in the reunited Church.

In its other use the interpretation of a Creed signifies ascertaining or exhibiting its own meaning *in se*—the precise substance of the doctrines which the Church anciently affirmed by means of it. The only freedom of interpretation in this sense which reasonable men will demand is freedom in the scholarly methods by which they ascertain what the Church really affirmed when it adopted the Creed. No doubt the interpreter will conclude that some phrases of the Creed are obviously metaphorical, such as ' right hand of the Father.' In such case, his interpretation will reckon with this. But he will not reach the real meaning of the Creed either if he treats its metaphors literally or its assertions of fact metaphorically ; and to reach the real meaning is the aim of the interpretation here referred to. If he does confuse metaphor and literal assertion, the result is not to be described as an exercise of freedom of interpretation but as a mistake.

The Modernist's demand for freedom in interpreting the Creeds involves an illegitimate use of the term interpret. He is really pleading for liberty to accept the Creeds in other than their actual meaning, other than that in which they have been accepted and prescribed by the Church, and to do so *without forfeiting the status of an official teacher of Church doctrine*. What he pleads for is not accurately described as freedom of interpretation but freedom to combat in the Church's pulpit certain doctrines contained in the Creeds. Such a plea cannot fail to be rejected by the ecumenical mind, by the reunited Church. And the oneness of mind which is the condition of genuine Christian unity obviously requires that ecumenical formularies shall be accepted by the Church's teachers in the sense in which the Church has imposed them. The reunited Church will often be discriminatingly merciful in discipline ; but it surely will not sanction the demand in question. Liberalism in the sense considered in these pages is hopelessly inconsistent with the reunion of Christendom.

(*b*) Only brief comment is needed on the statement in the Lausanne Report quoted above, alleging understanding ' that the several Churches will continue to make use of such special Confessions as they possess.' This is one of the specific affirmations in the Lausanne Reports which could not have been received *nem. con.* if it had been separately voted on instead of being merely an item in a Report of discussions which could not be completed for lack of time.

The freedom of provincial Churches to set forth definitions of doctrine to meet provincial needs or emergencies was exercised in the ancient Church, and under obvious limitations was generally acquiesced in. The limitations were that these definitions should neither enlarge, reduce, nor contradict the ecumenical Faith ; and that they should not displace ecumenical definitions. Such liberty is not likely to be refused in the reunited Church, for it is obviously necessary if provincial Churches are to fulfil their teaching office effectively.

But the language quoted seems to refer, can obviously be taken to refer, to Protestant Confessions of Faith. These differ in an important respect from the definitions of ancient provincial Councils. They are obviously *intended to differentiate denominational positions* ; and they supplement ecumenical doctrine by definitions which never can be recognised as in full harmony therewith. I think such a criticism can be made without committal to any specific attack upon their contents, and without going beyond undeniable historic facts. They certainly contain some definitions of theological value.

It should be clear that the doctrinal unity of the reunited Church cannot be maintained if Confessions of Faith are retained of differentiating purport—Confessions which are designed to crystallise and perpetuate positions incongruous with other Confessions of analogous origin and design. Confessions of such design and nature should give way to the aim of cultivating as far as possible one ecumenical mind. Unquestionably their continued use would be a cause of serious discord.

Behind this matter lies the subject of the continuance of denominational Churches and disciplines in the reunited Church universal. But it will have to be dealt with in a subsequent chapter (Chapter XII).

CHAPTER XI

AUTHORITY AND FREEDOM

HISTORY makes clear to all who are open to conviction that during the Middle Ages ecclesiastical authority in Western Christendom had been developed at the expense of Christian freedom, and had become a tyranny highly prejudicial to spiritual interests—even to secular welfare. The passion for freedom, both individual and social, which was a leading factor in the Protestant revolt, was an inevitable reaction from this tyranny, and cannot be justly condemned. But, as is apt to be the case with all reactionary movements, the revolt mentioned was not controlled by balanced judgment ; for excessive authority was replaced by excessive freedom from authority—from the authority divinely intended to be exercised by the Church universal. This involved the abandonment of certain vital things committed to the primitive Church for permanent stewardship and ministration, and therefore important spiritual losses.

It would seem that *the reformation needs completion by a restoration of the balance between authority and freedom*, equally upset by mediæval excesses of authority and by the passionate recoil which it naturally provoked. Such completion *will not be an undoing* of the reformation, *but a needed sequel* of it. And to appeal to the reformers in opposition to facing this need is to perpetuate the very onesidedness which inevitably attended their heroic revolt from the evils of their time. Their movement did not effect an ideal settlement, permanently to be protected from amendment, but was an explosive loosening of material from the quarry for subsequent deliberate finishing on lines of lasting beauty and meaning. Needless to say, without the restoration of balance of which I am writing there can be no reunion of Christendom—certainly not an enduring one. In this restoration of balance the excesses of hierarchical authority must also be eliminated, of course.

I. *Divine and Human Factors*

The problem of reunion, of the reunion which Christ wills, whereby all His earthly members of whatever present affiliation shall be effectively and visibly embraced in one flock, has no more central and pressing aspect than a workable adjustment of the claims of authority and of freedom. The fact that it is a thorny aspect of the problem, requiring care in handling, does not, however, alter the fact that it must be handled with frankness, as well as with mutual friendliness, if real advance is to be had toward that full reunion which the Spirit is moving many hearts and minds to promote. In the adjustment aimed at the fact should be kept in mind that, as in the secular order so in the spiritual, both freedom and authority have to be maintained in co-ordination, if the welfare of all is to be safeguarded. I mean freedom in relation to the individual and local, and authority in relation to orderly stability and unity and to common and mutual interests and relations.

In the great flock of Christ the social and the individual are mutually dependent; and according to the most ancient Christian tradition their co-ordination has been provided for by permanent divine arrangements—subject, indeed, to human abuse, but not rightly to be abandoned or substantially changed by human wills.

The reason why God has not left the business of co-ordinating these two factors in His Church to human wisdom as fully as in the civil sphere can be partly understood, perhaps, when we reckon with the great difference of function fulfilled by Church and State in the divine plan. The State has to do with the changing conditions and relations of this world, lying within human knowledge, and therefore properly left to human wisdom to reckon with. The State has problems to meet, but they belong entirely to the visible and temporal ; and a wise meeting of them may require very radical changes in the State itself. Beyond the broad purpose of conserving public order and temporal welfare, social and individual, the State has and needs no unchanging determinants ; and no factor in civil government can rightly be held to be permanently immune to change. Stability is indeed important, but in secular government this is at times dependent upon constitutional change.

On the other hand, the Church is charged with functions the nature and methods of which are determined by eternal interests ; and these interests are not, cannot be, fully made known to men or fully understood by them in this life. Behind the ministry and sacraments of the Church, behind the Church itself, lie unchanging divine mysteries, very imperfectly understood, but by which these things have to be controlled, if the spiritual ends in view are to be fulfilled with the fullest and most abiding success. The human conditions, under which they are to be fulfilled, do indeed change. They require, and in every age have secured, adjustments to meet them. But these adjustments have to be subject to considerations fully known to God alone, and to the consequent necessity of preserving without substantial change certain permanent arrangements for the ministry and sacraments of the Church on earth which, according to Catholic doctrine, God has made once for all.

One more point should be noted. We have no divine intimation that civil government in this world ought to be in the hands of one world-wide State, or to be conformed to one constitutional method. And the diversity in different lands of the conditions by which the methods of civil government have to be determined plainly preclude such unification. But God has unmistakably revealed His will that the Church should constitute one visible body and flock, a consummation which depends upon world-wide conformity of Christians to those elements of pastoral rule and sacramental ministration which are so widely believed to be divinely appointed.

II. *Authority*

Coming to consider severally the values and limits of authority and freedom in the Church, I take up authority first because in proper form it is the pre-condition of true freedom. Its restoration, with due safeguards against recurrence of its past excesses and abuses, is a *sine qua non* of ecumenical reunion. And, as has been indicated above, certain forms of authority will claim acceptance by the reunited Church, not only because of the primitive general belief in their divine appointment, still retained by a vast majority of Christians, but also because of the eternal and changeless interests which seem to have determined and fixed them.

I need not prove to the thoughtful and unprejudiced that some form of recognised authority is necessary in every social order, if true freedom is not to give way to anarchy. Law and order are essential to real liberty, and without authority law and order cannot be maintained. Furthermore, the unity of a social order depends upon unity in its authority, that is, upon common recognition of one authoritative government having jurisdiction coextensive with the whole society. And this holds true whatever may be the form of government accepted, whether autocracy, constitutional monarchy, or democracy.

This applies to the Church universal, which for effective unity must accept one ecumenical government, having jurisdiction, whatever its constitutional limits, wherever the united Church extends. Of course, such jurisdiction must be sufficiently limited to leave room for the necessary liberties of local Churches and of individual souls. Absolutism and comprehensive uniformity everywhere are out of question. But if real unity is to be preserved, the jurisdiction of ecumenical authority must be sufficiently effective throughout Christendom to secure general and visible conformity to whatever is held to be of divine appointment in ministry and sacraments, and to those elements of Eucharistic worship and spiritual discipline upon which depends the ability of all Christians to recognise and profitably to participate in a common spiritual fellowship and worship wherever they go.

In other words, the relations between ecumenical authority and the authority of particular or local Churches involve two requirements : that ecumenical authority should be visibly supreme ; and that the authority of particular Churches, within their several jurisdictions and so far as consistent with the common Faith and Order, should be safeguarded. In the fulfilment of these requirements, (a) ecumenical legislation will bind all ; but (b) the legislation of each particular Church, subject to this limitation, will bind those who are within its assigned jurisdiction ; and (c) both ecumenical and local authority will be maintained in such wise as to make their safeguarding of Faith, Order, and Unity minister also to the spiritual freedom of souls.

The ecumenical point of view is controlled by belief in divine appointment of the ancient threefold ministry, and will not permit acceptance of any form of ecclesiastical authority inconsistent with its God-given jurisdiction. This, however, is entirely consistent with the principle that ministerial authority may not become an external lordship, exercised independently of the approval of the faithful in general. And, in view of the lessons of experience, the participation of the laity in ecclesiastical branches of government should be constitutionalised, subject to acceptance of the God-given authority of the sacred ministry. There should also be an analogous constitutionalising of the respective functions of bishops and inferior clergy in ecclesiastical government. By constitutionalising I mean such canonical supplementing of divine appointments as will secure, under diverse and changing human conditions, the proper rights and liberties of all concerned.

That the reunited Church will be unable to legislate and maintain its unity, its law and order, without representative general assemblies or ecumenical councils of some kind is clear, and no particular Church or bishop should have a right either to interfere with their meeting, to tamper with their freedom, or to disregard the constitutional authority given them by the Church at large. It would be premature to speculate as to how the times of their meeting would be regulated, and as to their membership and procedure. But Catholic doctrine would require that the ancient pre-eminence of the episcopate in ecclesiastical rule, especially in matters of Christian Faith and Order, should be preserved in the constitution and methods of the Church's legislative assemblies. Local Churches would also require their own legislative bodies, in subordination to the ecumenical; and the principle of episcopal pre-eminence would have to be safeguarded in them also.

III. *As to the Roman Primacy*

If ecumenical authority is to maintain itself, its continuity must be preserved; and this clearly requires that, subject to the legislative authority just considered, there must be some central machinery for the administration of ecumenical affairs. The modern Continuation Committee illustrates in its special sphere the need to which I refer. The Church's general interests will often suffer damage unless their everyday care is provided for. The Roman See has claimed to be the divinely appointed agent for fulfilling this need, and has gradually magnified its office. To-day the papal claim, accepted with varying degrees of understanding and assurance by the largest Christian Communion, includes immediate jurisdiction in every diocese of Christendom, and infallibility, apart from the subsequent consent of the Church, in all *ex cathedra* determinations in doctrine and morals. The supremacy of General Councils over the Papal See is rejected.

Needless to say, the non-Roman portions of Christendom regard the Vatican Claims as a human development; as justified neither by divine appointment nor by acceptance at any time by the universal Church; as fostering corruption; and as subversive of Christian liberties. I need not discuss these claims here. The pertinent questions are whether the Roman See can be sufficiently reformed and limited in its claims and functions to gain ecumenical approval; and whether in that event the united Church can safely, and ought to, recognise that See, under proper constitutional safeguards, as the proper agent of ecumenical business as above described.

Papal defenders say that, being based upon divine appointment, the Vatican claims cannot be reversed or reduced, and that submission to them is the necessary basis of unity. Protestants, of course, deny such divine appointment. But they usually deny also that the Papacy can be acceptably reformed, apparently forgetting the resources of overruling providence and the fact that only the divine will is immune to change. Catholics other than Roman agree with Protestants in rejecting the Vatican claims, but disagree with both Roman Catholics and Protestants in that they believe in the possibility of their proper abatement. In this connection it is to be remembered that an undefined Roman primacy—not the *jurisdictional supremacy* of later days—was accepted by the whole ancient Church. At Chalcedon it was acknowledged, and at least rhetorically linked up with the generally believed Petrine origin of the

Roman See. There is still very considerable Catholic agreement outside the Roman obedience that a certain primacy pertains to the Roman See ' by divine providence.' Important writers go further and say, ' by divine appointment.' But all non-Roman Catholics agree, (a) that the existing papal system substantially enlarges the primacy anciently accepted ; (b) that it is a non-primitive development ; (c) that it is human, and therefore open to change ; (d) that it is ecclesiastically illegitimate, because never obtaining that ecumenical acceptance upon which depends the legitimacy of local claims affecting the whole Church.

My reason for giving space to the subject of the Roman See is that full Christian reunion cannot be had without a generally accepted settlement of the question of papal authority and incidentally of the future executive machinery for the everyday handling of ecumenical business. The subject cannot be ignored helpfully by students of the reunion problem in any section of Christendom, Catholic or Protestant ; and hasty radical conclusions will not avail.

If non-Roman Christendom is wrong and existing papal claims are valid, the sooner our studies lead us to accept the Roman method of reunion and submit to the Roman See the better. But even if they represent in their present climax an illegitimate development, purely human and fruitful in obscurantism and spiritual tyranny, certain vital questions remain for all of us who take this view but perceive the need of full Christian reunion : (a) Ought the anciently accepted Roman primacy to be continued in the reunited Church ? The question has both doctrinal and practical aspects ; (b) Can the existing papal system, and the claims connected therewith, be outgrown, reformed, and constitutionally safeguarded against recurring danger, in such wise as to justify an acceptance of Roman primacy by the reunited Church ? (c) If not, what alternative can be adopted ?

To Protestants and to many Anglicans the reform

referred to in the second question seems clearly impossible, and they would therefore say ' No ' to the first question. I am pleading for reconsideration of the possibility of papal reformation. We believe that the papal accretions in need of reform are human and therefore not immune to change. Of course, if the anciently accepted Roman primacy itself is purely human, and under all safeguards is inevitably subject to corrupt development, we may reasonably believe that the future changes which no human system can escape will result in the final extinction of Roman primacy rather than in the reform of existing papalism.

(*a*) Assuming that the Roman primacy, even in its anciently accepted form, is of human origin, it is not necessarily evil *in se*, unsuitable for permanent providential use, and insusceptible under divine overruling of reformation when in need thereof.

(*b*) The widespread belief that the Roman primacy, whether of formal divine appointment or not, came into existence by divine providence and is intended of God to continue in the Church, does not exempt it from the need of reformation, but does suggest both the possibility and likelihood of such event.

(*c*) The current absolutism of the utterances of the Vatican and of Roman controversial writers increasingly betrays the temper which attends anxiety as to the security of the position affirmed. There are many indications in uncontroversial Roman literature of an openness of mind to non-Roman and modern ideas which is incongruous with the Vatican mentality and claims. The general mental atmosphere of the Roman Communion has been changing for some time, and in a direction which must ultimately make Vatican claims a patent anachronism. In time, I do not say soon, Vaticanism will have to yield to the growing intelligence of its own world-wide constituency.

(*d*) The resources of divine providence have to be reckoned with. The slow and unobserved processes of human minds, we know, are sometimes very suddenly revealed in startling results, precipitated by some turn of events or change of situation. So it may happen that some divinely overruled cataclysm, whether in the international or the intellectual field, will precipitate a changed Christian outlook which will make the reformation in question and world-wide Christian reunion both possible and inevitable.

Whatever may be the force of these considerations, the need of full reunion, and the absurdity of such reunion with the Roman Communion left out, plainly demand of us the most patient study of the problem of including that Communion in the reunion for which we labour.

IV. *Freedom*

In trying to make clear the place of ecumenical authority in the Church, even in those parts of my argument which will seem most remote to Protestants, I have assumed, and now reassert, that the test which authority must meet in the reunited Church is its practical harmony with true Christian freedom, the freedom of particular parts of the Church and of individual souls. I assume and assert that neither true authority nor true freedom can either develop rightly or maintain itself permanently apart from the other.

I do not need here to treat of the manifold conceptions and technical definitions of ' freedom ' and ' liberty.' It is sufficient to say that what I am considering in this section consists of such established conditions and rights, whether of individual Christians or of provincial Churches, as permit and facilitate all lines of unhampered—I do not mean irresponsible—inquiry, conviction, expression, conduct, and local usage or prescription which are consistent with loyalty to the essential Faith and Order of the Christian Church, and with maintenance of its corporate unity, world-wide fellowship and spiritual welfare.

I believe that such freedom is necessary for the

fulfilment of God's plan in establishing His Church, and for the ultimate spiritual welfare both of individual souls and of the fellowship in which God wills to save them and bring them to Himself. It is evidently a conditioned freedom ; but in no sphere of human life is unconditional freedom either defensible or possible to cultivate without the destruction of all real freedom. I think that reflecting Protestants as well as Catholics will accept this general premise, whether they agree in their method of applying it to the current Christian situation or not. It is the truth which makes men free ; and this means that the conditions which facilitate its acquisition, and the institutions and practices, whether social or individual, which are believed to be dictated by it, cannot consistently or safely be rejected or neglected by intelligent cultivators of liberty.

It is the truth that makes men free ; and private judgment, whether intelligently exercised or not, is in every case the mental act by which individual seekers after truth obtain convictions concerning it, and concerning the theoretical implications and practical obligations involved in it. Moreover, this judgment ought to be unhampered ; but unhampered does not mean unconditioned, individualistic, unreasoning, or irresponsible. Such types of private judgment go astray, and do not favour enjoyment of that high spiritual freedom which a proper and comprehensive assimilation and application of Christian truth affords.

In Protestant use the phrase ' private judgment ' has meant judgment which is independent of ecclesiastical authority. That is, it presupposes a previous private judgment, adverse to the Church's teaching authority, that the Scriptures are the sole source and rule of faith. Of course, as thus understood, Catholics are led to repudiate private judgment, meaning judgment which refuses to reckon with Catholic doctrine. But, apart from such polemical use and association, and properly understood, both Protestant and Catholic believers owe their several systems of belief and practice to private judgment—to personally attained conviction. Its exercise leads a Protestant to resort to Scripture alone, but leads a Catholic to judge that the Church is the divinely appointed and most competent available teacher of divine truth, the proper use of Scripture being to test and confirm Church teaching. Upon this initial act of private judgment his subsequent judgments as to the several doctrines and consequent prescriptions of the Church are logically based, as logically as any conclusion is deduced from its premises.

To pursue the logic of initial private judgment in this manner is not to abandon mental freedom, but is to think consistently and responsibly. No thoughtful person will defend the proposition that free thinking means illogical thinking, that is, refusal to accept the rational consequences of one's primary judgments and convictions. And this applies to the general working system of religious life which is deduced from these convictions, whether Protestant or Catholic.

To live according to Catholic convictions may involve forms of restraint and obedience which to the Protestant mind appears to be contrary to liberty. But those who freely will to obey the truth do not feel deprived of freedom in submitting to the discipline involved. They feel that they are entering into the liberty of the children of God. It is disbelief in the Catholic premises, and consequent repulsion from Catholic ideals, which make submission to Catholic doctrines and prescriptions seem like abandonment of mental and spiritual freedom. If Protestants came to understand and believe in the Catholic system the Catholic discipline would seem to them to afford necessary conditions of freedom. We all argue that the way to the perfect freedom of the world to come is that of abandonment of self-will, that of self-surrender.

The fact remains that the premises which severally determine the subsequent judgments of Protestants and

Catholics need testing. It is truth rather than subjective opinion that makes us free. The fact also remains that every system is liable to human abuse, and mediæval abuses within Western Christendom were prejudicial to Christian liberty. The premises—rules of faith—referred to call for fresh study, and the reformation of mediæval abuses must be completed. What I plead for is that we should transcend provincial outlooks, and acquire ecumenical largeness of mind.

I have considered certain aspects of the subject of this chapter in other parts of the volume ; but, of course, I do not pretend to have discussed ' authority and freedom ' adequately, either here or there. I have had to content myself with punctuating a few significant aspects of the subject which become prominent when it is viewed ' in ecumenical light,' the light in which I am urging my readers to view every branch of the problem of unity.

One more point, which I have no space to discuss, appears to call for attention at this moment, when prominent Nonconformists have been concerning themselves with the revision of The English Church Prayer Book. The point is that the plea for spiritual freedom applies in the Catholic direction as well as in the Evangelical. There are Catholic liberties as well as Protestant ; and reunion between an undivided Anglican Communion and non-episcopal Churches is a practical impossibility unless they are protected.

CHAPTER XII

DENOMINATIONALISM

It is not a necessary requirement of reunion that its participants should commit themselves one way or the other as to the necessity and consequent justification of denominationalism *under the circumstances of its development in the past*. That sincere ministers and members of modern denominations have been blessed of God in their labours and lives is not disputed. And if many Christians believe that the *permanent continuance* of such denominations is inconsistent with the plan of God for His Church, this does not necessarily imply condemnation of those who have adhered to them in the past. In labour for reunion it is wisest, most Christian and safest to forget the troublous past, as far as possible, and only to consider the future, or the requirements for permanent and wholesome reunion. Thus also the interests of love, the very bond of peace, will be protected from the dangers of useless controversy. No section of Christendom can fully justify its record, and none is capable of judging the records of other sections without error. All need to repent, and all need to let judging alone. The questions of Faith and Order which have to be settled in order to bring about true unity can, by the grace of God, be faced and settled, without formulating either favourable or unfavourable pronouncements as to past movements. In this great matter our task is to remove the existing causes of Christian divisions, and to discuss them only for that purpose, with mutual love and forbearance.

I. *Can it Continue after Reunion ?*

The question to be considered is whether denominations, in the usual meaning of that term, can be perpetuated either rightly or safely in reunited Christendom. If it be granted that the accomplishment of reunion may require transitional and temporary accommodations to denominational needs, the question of perpetuation remains to be considered. And this requires prayerful study both of divine appointments and of other practically necessary requirements of effective and permanent reunion. Moreover, we should realise the importance of such reunion, and be led thereby to resist the desire to save any other faces than that of the united Church of God. Loyalty to existing denominations while they continue, and refusal to doubt the blessings received in them, cannot rightly be condemned. But such dispositions are entirely consistent with the future changes that may be necessary for the reunion of Christendom, even if they involve the discontinuance of denominations. That is, of particular Churches retaining mutually incongruous confessional positions, jurisdictional polities, sacramental usages, and spiritual disciplines.

In final issue, then, can denominational Churches of the diverse types above indicated, be co-ordinated within reunited Christendom, without sacrificing the required interior fellowship and the larger spiritual blessings which, from the nature of things and by the will of God, depend thereupon? Certain degrees of variation in non-essentials as between provincial and national Churches have always been recognised by Catholic consent to be necessary and allowable. And the same consent has been given to the organisation of religious orders and other societies, devoted to special aims and designed to satisfy special temperaments and needs, provided they have not been set up as 'Churches' or jurisdictional parts, as such, of the universal Church. But the question with which this paragraph begins,

when considered in ecumenical light, is certain to
receive a negative answer; and several controlling
reasons for such answer ought to be reckoned with.
In particular :

(a) Every arrangement in particular Churches which
is certain to be misunderstood by Christians elsewhere,
and cause mutual suspicion between the Churches,
should be avoided as far as possible. The irremovable
linguistic, racial, climatic, and national differences with
consequent necessary local adjustments, make the
maintenance of real spiritual unity difficult in any case.
Indeed, they make it impossible, unless care is exercised
to preserve as full and visible family resemblance
between the Churches as human nature and unavoidable
exigencies permit.

(b) The retention of existing denominational Confessions of Faith, or the framing of new ones, would
certainly be objectionable to the ecumenical mind.
Existing Confessions reveal important divergences in
doctrine, divergences leading to mutual suspicions of
orthodoxy. The fact that considerable *theological* divergences in a world-wide Christendom are inevitable is
clear, and for the universal Church to exercise nervous
watchfulness over theological developments would be
inconsistent with vital mental freedom. Furthermore,
the freedom of particular Churches to make doctrinal
pronouncements in emergency cannot be limited beyond the
requirement of common and unreserved acceptance of
the ecumenical Creeds, without seriously handicapping
the teaching function of these Churches. But the need
of a mutually recognised unity of Faith seems plainly to
require that no *formal Creed or Confession of Faith* should
be prescribed in any part of reunited Christendom which
is not imposed by ecumenical authority. The experience
of centuries shows that the multiplication of dogmatic
definitions is prejudicial both to unity of Faith and to the
mental liberty upon which *vital* conviction depends.
Modern denominational Confessions need not be

repudiated, but they should be treated as historical documents, no longer to be imposed upon consciences.

(c) The experience of several centuries shows that denominational distinctions, both in inception and in subsequent working, are so far separative *in se* that they preclude development of that common interior fellowship which is the paramount aim, condition, and necessary mark of real unity—of the unity for which the Lord prayed. In a truly united Christendom loyal believers ought to be able, wherever they go, to recognise the supremacy of their own fundamental Faith and Order, and to feel spiritually at home. The modern increase of travel accentuates this.

The Protestant's emphatic disapproval of uniformity is justifiable in so far as he has in view certain excessive and tyrannical forms of it, excessive in non-essential details and tyrannical in the manner of its imposition and enforcement. But the securing of such uniformity in the reunited Church is so plainly impossible and contrary to past ecumenical practice that fears of attempts to establish it in that Church are unwarranted. The conformity required for unity is one of essential Faith and Order, and of such visible harmony in the methods of corporate Eucharistic worship and sacramental life as will enable ordinary folk to *see* that the common fellowship is real and abiding.

To paraphrase a well-known saying—In things generally deemed essential either to Christianity, as such, or to visible unity, a manifest unity and generic likeness ; In things neither thus essential nor necessary for visible unity, liberty ; In all things, notable care to maintain visible charity between all sections of Christendom.

The conclusion to which these considerations point is that *the perpetuation of denominational autonomies and variations of the kind and degree here under discussion will absolutely preclude the full unity of Christendom for which we labour and pray ; and is certain permanently to be unacceptable to the ecumenical mind.* The vital things in need of preservation, for which the denominations severally stand, should not be lost ; but if they are to be preserved *in just proportions* and without baneful caricature, the separative method of denominationalism must give way to unitive and ecumenically acceptable methods. And denominational organisation must so far give way as to secure common acceptance and supremacy everywhere of one ministry, one general method of distributing local ecclesiastical jurisdiction, and a degree of conformity in the midst of variety which will visibly manifest the *corporate* unity of Christendom and the substantial sameness everywhere of its fundamental Faith and Order. Is this possible ? It is possible just so far as permanent and wholesome ecumenical unity is possible. Such unity is no doubt difficult, and to be achieved only through protracted study, prayer, and effort. But God wills it, and that constitutes a proof of possibility.

II. *Will its Abandonment Imperil Vital Principles?*

The mutual incompatibility between denominationalism and full Christian unity which I have been endeavouring to make clear raises an important question, quite too important to be ignored. It is widely urged that the several modern denominations have recovered, and stand for, certain vital principles and interests which before their organisation had become widely obscured and disregarded in Western Christendom, and which still lack adequate recognition within the Churches from which they separated. Unless, therefore, sufficient provisions are made in the reunited universal Church for their practical observance and safeguarding, it is argued, an abandonment of denominational autonomies would constitute a surrender of these principles and interests—a culpable breach of trust. The question, then, is this : Can the vital things for which the several modern denominations stand be safely turned over to the reunited Church for the practically effective maintenance which they demand in an adequate Christian system ?

To define in detail, and to estimate the values of, the principles for which the several denominations claim to stand is unnecessary for my general argument. Therefore I content myself with broad acknowledgments. Certain of these principles are indeed vital, recognised theoretically at least to be so by Christians of every name ; and they will have to be safeguarded practically in the reunited Church. Furthermore, this safeguarding will require the preservation of just balance between authority and liberty, as has been indicated more fully in the previous chapter—authority in the interest of united fellowship and the common Faith and Order, and liberty in the interest of adjustment to local and temporal conditions and of unhampered inquiry and personal religion. Still further, it is certain that much remains to be accomplished by way of abatement of local claims on the Catholic side, as well as recovery in pure forms by Protestants of those elements of Christian Faith and Order which they have abandoned because of the corrupting accretions which obscured their true nature and necessity.

The question then is, Can denominationalism in the sense of this chapter be altogether abandoned for the sake of real, visible, and corporate unity and fellowship without compromise or surrender of vital principles ? I do not see how anyone who thoughtfully considers the nature of the unity which God wills for His Church can answer this question otherwise than with an unqualified affirmative. What God wills is obviously paramount in determining our duty ; and if the unity which He wills requires, as I have given reasons for believing, an abandonment of denominational autonomies, we may be sure that He will somehow enlighten those concerned as to how this requirement can be fulfilled by them without compromise or surrender of any vital Christian principle. But a certain venture of faith will be involved, of course, and genuine self-effacement. Such is the cost of any great spiritual achievement.

III. *Pertinent Considerations*

I have maintained that we are at the educational stage of labour for the reunion of all Christendom, and that attempts to formulate final ' terms ' and schematic details for its consummation are now hopelessly premature. Therefore, I have not ventured to predict how the safeguarding of the principles referred to in the previous chapter will be provided for in the reunited universal Church. When Christians are really ready for reunion, provincial outlooks of every kind will have been transcended, and proper methods of action will emerge which our present differences hinder us from perceiving and approving. Yet it is consistent with what I am saying to contribute a few thoughts, not of schematic definition, but designed to show that the difficulties which now exclude the reunion of Catholic and Protestant Communions from the field of practical politics need not be regarded as permanently insuperable.

(*a*) The truth is mighty and will ultimately prevail among all who self-effacingly make its attainment paramount. Accordingly, all the oppositions of doctrine between Catholics and Protestants will in time be removed : partly by more earnest study of the questions involved, now plainly increasing ; partly by the lapse of time and dying out of sixteenth-century tempers ; partly by the cosmopolitan widening of intelligence, visibly affecting even the most obscurantist parts of Christendom ; partly by great changes of external nature, certain to develop a new general outlook and bring new mental and spiritual perspectives ; but especially by overruling providence and enlightening guidance of the Spirit of truth, made effective by prayer and consequent spiritual docility. If we exercise our imaginations sufficiently, and keep in mind both the vast resourcefulness of God and the changes which preclude the permanent continuance of human provincialisms in any one stay, we shall perceive the rashness of negative dogmatism concerning the possibility of ultimate agreement between sincere Christians as to the things which have to be safeguarded in Christ's reunited Church.

(b) The blind alleys into which present-day conferences appear to run, as soon as they seriously face the deeper issues involved—for example, those in Great Britain between representatives of the Lambeth Conference and of the Free Churches, and those between Romans and Anglicans at Malines—while they reveal obstacles not now removable, also reveal tempers and aims which are new and potential of growth which the most militant sections on either side cannot stop. The very form and tone of recent extreme utterances, official and unofficial, in the Roman Communion, reveal an uneasy sense of growing disposition among its intelligent members to reinterpret, and to reckon fairly with non-Roman Christendom. That a certain degree of reformation of sixteenth-century abuses has occurred in the Roman Church is evident to unprejudiced historical students. What is less widely realised, and denied by papal controversialists, is that the whole mental outlook of educated Roman Catholics is changing and becoming less and less absolute. The saying that Rome cannot change is contradicted both by the law that only the divine is immune to change and by the facts of history.

(c) ‘ Caricature,’ unintentional of course, is a proper description of the formulations of truth and principle whereon provincial and denominational Churches rest their case for separation from other Churches. And it is practically impossible to maintain any particular truth or principle in just proportions, and with due regard for the fullness of Christian truth and grace, when given the one-sided emphasis which it necessarily receives in a separative propaganda. If the vital principles for which the separate sections of Christendom now stand are to be maintained in proper perspectives, that is, truly, they must be maintained in one fellowship and in the context of the whole Christian Faith and Order. It is no more possible to find in a denominational formula the right proportions of truth than it is possible rightly to describe the side of a triangle when taken away from the rest of the triangle. To the most careful scrutiny it is then only a straight line. The terms of reunion may be beyond predicting now, but the interests of truth require that it shall put an end to *separate* denominational contentions and outlooks. This does not mean that special emphasis upon particular truths, principles, and usages designed to meet local or exigent conditions and needs can rightly be discouraged in the reunited Church. It means that such emphasis and variation shall be safeguarded from resulting in separative and one-sided developments by a felt ecumenical background—a background that cannot be either realised or maintained on the denominational basis which I have been discussing.

(*d*) I have already referred to religious Orders and other organisations, found in both Catholic and Protestant Churches, and open to increase in number and variety, as affording means for promoting special aims, and for meeting the needs of special temperaments, without involving disregard of previously existing ecclesiastical allegiance and fellowship in faith, worship, and discipline. I desire to call attention to the opportunities thus available for emphasis upon truths and practices requiring it, and for supplementary methods of devotion and spiritual exercise such as cannot rightly be prescribed for all the faithful. It is, of course, necessary for unity that these methods should be supplementary. They should not be substitutes for the common Eucharistic worship by which the one fellowship is visibly expressed and held in one, in obedience to divine and apostolic prescription. The same need of keeping unity intact will require that these organisations and methods shall not represent *divisive aims*; and that, while given room

for spontaneous development and free action, they shall
be amenable to such ecclesiastical oversight as may be
necessary for preserving the common discipline.   That
special movements, when wholly exempt from responsibility to authority, tend to get disastrously out of hand
has frequently been demonstrated in the past.

*The paramount need of Christianity to-day is the restoration of
genuine, visible, and abiding unity of all Christendom*—a unity
which cannot be had without the surrender of divisive
organisations, ecclesiastical and other, to one world-wide
and visible *ecclesia*.   No one who transcends a provincial
outlook can regard any other method of remedy for the
existing futilities as adequate.   And those who think the
problem through must finally perceive that, in spite of
the minor evils which will in any case continue to exist
within the Church on earth, no really vital interest or
principle can be safeguarded justly, and with due regard
for the wholeness of Christian truth and practice, except
from the ecumenical standpoint of an effectively united
universal Church.   It is to such solution of existing
disorders that the Holy Spirit is now calling us all.

However long the process of fulfilling the task
involved may prove to be, no degree of self-effacement
and of patience in loving reconsideration, prayer, and
effort is too great for acceptance by those to whom the
call has come.   God wills it ; and His grace and overruling providence will surely enable Christians to perform it.   It depends, therefore, upon our self-surrender,
our unqualified willingness to obey the divine call
regardless of costs, and our patient perseverance, in the
face of many passing setbacks, in a very long task.

CHAPTER XIII

TWO CURRENT MOVEMENTS

I HAD intended to end my book with the previous chapter; but, while I have been writing, two movements have matured which seem likely to result in somewhat radical proposals being submitted to the Lambeth Conference of 1930. These movements and proposals bear directly on the standpoint and central contentions of this book, and I feel that my work will not be complete without some consideration of their nature and bearing on the problem of full Christian union.

I. *Mutual Recognition of Ministries*

I consider first the movement determinedly promoted by the widely respected and energetic bishop of Gloucester, Dr. Headlam, for a mutual recognition of validity between episcopal and non-episcopal ministries, with agreement that thenceforth all ordinations in the united Church shall be episcopally performed. It is reported that this plan, or something like it, will be presented for approval to the Lambeth Conference. The main pleas are two.

(*a*) The first is practical, that unless some relaxation is offered of the present requirement that *existing* non-episcopal ministers must be episcopally ordained in order to be given recognition, and to be permitted to minister, in the Anglican Communion, there is no hope of reunion between the Anglican Church and the Free

Churches of Great Britain.   There are several practical
and conclusive reasons for maintaining that the proposed
course has insuperable difficulties.

1. If carried through, it would certainly provoke
schism in the Anglican Communion.   It would involve
for a generation the corporate allowance of celebrations
of the Holy Eucharist within the united Church by
ministers having no episcopal ordination, a result which,
as Bishop Gore rightly declared several years ago, would
split the English Church in twain.   The fact is that, in
common with the major part of Christendom, a large
section of the Anglican Communion, a section not
confined to those called Anglo-Catholics, is firmly convinced of the invalidity of non-episcopal exercise of
priestly functions.   And they definitely repudiate any
method of removing this invalidity other than that of
episcopal ordination.   Surely a schism-provoking procedure is not conducive to unity.

2. The likelihood of acceptance of such a scheme by
the Free Churches themselves seems very remote so long
as these Churches are unable to reach true organic union
between themselves—a fact which shows that the
question of valid ordination, not in controversy between
these Churches, is not the only barrier to reunion which
has to be reckoned with.

3. And, if there are other barriers to reunion between
Churches within the Nonconformist group, the same is
true as between these Churches and the Anglican, along
with the fact that the Anglican Communion is committed
to various essential elements of the Catholic system which
Nonconformists repudiate.   I need not try to list them,
but the outstanding barrier lies in the field of doctrine—
the indisputable fact that much Catholic teaching retained
in the Anglican Prayer Book, and regarded widely among
us as having vital practical implications, is repudiated by
Nonconformists.   Many Anglicans would feel certain
that if in their present state of conviction Nonconformists
were united with them in one Church, sooner or later the

official doctrine of the Anglican Communion would be modified in vital particulars.

4. Finally, if, in spite of these apparently insuperable difficulties, the Home Reunion scheme referred to were achieved, and the Anglican Communion as a whole involved therein, the result could not constitute a step towards the reunion of Christendom at large. On the contrary, for the reasons specified in paragraphs 1 and 3 above, it would raise new obstacles. It would nullify the part which the Anglican Church is striving to fulfil in uniting Catholics and Protestants, and would identify that Church finally with the Protestant group of Churches in the conviction of the whole Catholic world—Eastern Orthodox as well as Roman.

These reasons serve to confirm the general position taken in this book, that true and abiding reunion of Christendom must be based upon the ancient Catholic Faith and Order, and that reunion between Protestants and an undivided Anglican Communion cannot be had on any other basis. Progress towards reunion in this direction waits on education, and on its bringing about common acceptance of the Catholic system in Faith and Order.

(b) The second argument is theoretical, consisting of a denial of any ancient authority for the doctrine of apostolic succession, with the deduction that, whatever may be the practical reasons for restoring episcopal ordination throughout Christendom, we ought not to impose as condition of reunion the acceptance of belief in apostolic succession as being essential to ecclesiastical continuity, and as confining to the episcopal order the power of validly ordaining the Church's ministers.

Before answering this, it seems well to comment on a recently reported statement by the Bishop of Gloucester, that the doctrine of apostolic succession to which he took exception was ' that grace was transmitted by what might be called the mechanical laying-on of hands from

generation to generation.' If his words were correctly
reported they reveal a strange misunderstanding of the
doctrine in question. In Catholic theology it is a truism
that the earthly minister of a sacrament, in particular of
ordination, is *not the source or channel* of its grace. He is
merely the agent appointed to fulfil in Christ's name the
sacramental conditions under which Christ wills to
impart grace *from Himself*, by the operation of the Holy
Spirit. No transmission of grace from one generation
to another is supposed by Catholic theologians to be
achieved through the laying-on of hands in apostolic
succession. What is thereby transmitted is the ministerial
office, or the *authority to minister* in Christ's name. The
grace bestowed in the sacrament of Holy Order comes not
from the earthly ordainer or consecrator, but from the
Lord Himself. The Catholic doctrine of apostolic succession affirms two things : that the earthly ministerial
authority originally given by Christ to the Apostles,
being given in terms of perpetuity, requires uninterrupted
transmission ; and that the only agency for its valid
transmission is the episcopal order.

I return to the Bishop's denial of ancient authority for
this doctrine, the gist of which is the contention that
the ' succession ' passages in early writers depended upon
for its support do not refer to succession by ordination,
but to succession in apostolic sees. These sees are said
to have had a continuous succession of bishops from
apostolic times, but the assertion that each occupant
of a particular see was consecrated by his predecessor
in the succession referred to is neither made nor credible.
In brief, the modern assertion of the fact and necessity
of an apostolic succession by episcopal ordinations is
lacking in ancient writers.

We must admit, of course, that the ancient use of the
phrase ' apostolic succession ' did not mean succession
by ordination, but succession in office, a use of terms
which does not by itself establish the doctrine now signi-
fied by that phrase. But, as is clearly shown by Dr. C. H.

Turner, in the third of the ' Essays on the Early History
of the Church and the Ministry,' edited by the late
Dr. H. B. Swete, the evidence that the doctrine under
discussion was held by the ancient Church is more conclusive than Dr. Headlam's emphasis on the non-
antiquity of our present use of the phrase ' apostolic
succession ' permits him to perceive. As against the
subversive developments of Gnosticism, and the claim
that it represented the true sequel of apostolic teaching,
the Fathers appealed to the genuine apostolic tradition
contained in the Creed and the Scriptures and from
apostolic days officially transmitted without interruption
by the *successive* bishops of the apostolic sees. But there
is abundant evidence that, in order to be recognised by
the Church as validly possessed of this succession, each
of the bishops not only had to be lawfully chosen by
the local Church concerned, but also had ' to be lawfully
entrusted with the *charisma* of the episcopate by the
ministry of those already recognised as possessing it.'
(Cf. *op. cit.*, pp. 107 f.) The universal requirement of
episcopal ordination, coupled with the emphasis on continuity in the Church's hierarchy, clearly shows that
what is meant by apostolic succession to-day was not
less emphatically held by the ancients to be vital, although
they used different language. In this connection it seems
worth while to call attention to two passages in Bishop
Headlam's ' The Doctrine of the Church and Christian
Reunion ' (1920).

   1. On page 73 of that book, after emphasising the
fact that the circumstances of the organisation of the
Church at Jerusalem by the Apostles were abnormal,
and could not be repeated, he says, ' But at the same
time the organisation of the Church at Jerusalem suggests an exact resemblance to that in later days of bishop,
presbyter, and deacon ; and it is not improbable that
that model assisted in building up the later organisation
of the Church.' That the conditions were abnormal is
at once true and non-significant for the argument. They

were abnormal and unique because initial. The Church's organisation was being *created*, and had to be developed under exigent pioneer conditions, overruled by the guiding Spirit in such wise as to establish what Dr. Headlam suggests was taken by post-apostolic Christians to be the ' model ' for imitation by other Churches—as rapidly, I add, as their maturity of development fitted them to be given local autonomy. It should also be added that as the mother Church, and as organised by the consentient authority of the Apostles—forewarned by Christ, according to Clement, to make provision for continuance of the oversight—the Church of Jerusalem was rightly regarded by the post-apostolic Church as the authoritative norm of ecclesiastical organisation.

2. On pages 131–132, *op. cit.*, the Bishop says, ' There are a considerable number of instances quoted of ordination by other than bishops. None of them are conclusive, but there are, I think, signs that the rule had not been always rigidly or universally observed.' In other words, he reveals his inability to find *conclusive proof* that non-episcopal ordination was ever permitted or recognised as valid by the ancient Church. The cases to which he refers in footnotes have been repeatedly shown to be susceptible of interpretation in harmony with the requirement of episcopal ordination ; and there is no trace of the disturbance that would certainly have arisen if this requirement had upset a previous allowance of non-episcopal ordination.

II. *The South Indian Proposal*

Any of my readers who attended the Lausanne Conference will readily recall the burning words with which Bishop Tubbs of Tinnevelly pleaded for some *action* by the Conference looking to hastening of reunion. Also there was the pathetic presentation by Bishop Azariah of Dornakal of the peculiar difficulties encountered by missionaries in India because of Christian divisions.   In ultimate spiritual analysis, the evils of division are as serious at home as they are in the mission field ; but they are more visible to all there, and, speaking from the missionaries' practical standpoint, Bishop Tubbs was right in saying that the movement towards reunion was more urgent among those labouring in India than at home.   Accordingly, we may not disregard Bishop Azariah's plea for patience at their lack of interest in bygone controversies in view of the vital need of reunion as soon as possible which insistently obtrudes itself upon their attention.   The obstinate fact remains, alas ! that reunion pushed through under emotional stress, and leaving unremedied divergences of mind which are certain to engender friction in daily religious life, will not cure the evils of division, but will end sooner or later in renewed schism and increased exasperation. Things believed to be essential to the Christian system, and which determine the visible methods of religious life, cannot be combined in an organic fellowship with arrangements that give authorised sanction to conflicting beliefs and practices.   Moreover, a union in India which violates the convictions of home Churches in matters deemed vital by them must under any circumstances be regarded as an unjustifiable snatching at a doubtfully working local advantage at the cost of putting back the general cause of Christian unity.

The fact that the South Indian scheme is not yet finally adopted, and may be subjected to important modifications in response to the criticisms which it is receiving, should, of course, be borne in mind in reckoning with it.   None the less, it is being pushed with very serious intent by responsible parties ; and no just complaint can be made against definite expression of sincere adverse judgments as to its proposals.   We are all vitally concerned in matters which obviously affect the problem of the reunion of Christendom at large, and have the right to discuss them, not less so because we ought to do so patiently, discriminatingly, and kindly.

The aspects of the scheme, if adopted, which most obviously complicate the wider problems of the reunion of Christendom at large, and are most directly open to adverse criticism from the Catholic and Anglican standpoint, are the following :

1. The absence of any other than a practical or opportunist basis for acceptance of the episcopate, coupled with the episcopate's acceptance of stipulations which sanction distinctively Protestant principles ;

2. Recognition for thirty years, at least, of existing Protestant ministers, not episcopally ordained, as ministers of the Word and Sacraments *of* the United Church, and sanction of the reception of Communion at their hands by any of the members of the United Church ;

3. The provision that, after the above-mentioned period of thirty years, the United Church ' will consider and decide the question of . . . exceptions to the general principle of an episcopally-ordained ministry '— a provision which clouds with doubt any effective fulfilment of the avowed intention that ultimately the ministry of the United Church shall be wholly of episcopal ordination ;

4. The proposed union being made possible by separation between the Anglican dioceses of North and South India respectively—' the absence of any organic union with the Northern Province being accepted temporarily for the sake of unity ' ;

5. The attempt to maintain open communion of the United Church with all the respective home Churches with which the several bodies participating in the union have hitherto been in communion ;

6. The incidental hope that the bishops of the United Church will continue to be admitted to the Lambeth Conferences ; and, *at the same time*, that affiliation may be granted to the United Church by the World Presby-

terian Alliance, the World Union of Congregational Churches, and the Œcumenical Methodist Conference ;

7. The allowance of forms previously sanctioned by the several uniting Churches for admission to full membership in the United Church as alternatives to episcopal Confirmation—thereby sanctioning the interpretation of Confirmation as *merely* a form of such admission, and putting aside the Catholic and Anglican doctrine thereof.

The impression produced by these particulars is definitely cumulative. It may, of course, be objected that each should be considered separately, on its own merits, but they are very evidently interrelated. They cannot be adequately understood except as hanging together, and as involving an interconnected series of formal concessions to anti-Catholic positions. If adopted, they will have influence in weakening Catholic requirements at home, and will imperil the Catholic status of the Anglican Communion at large, if that Communion acquiesces in their adoption. Moreover, they represent compromises between conflicting principles, and preclude any full corporate maintenance in the United Church of the ancient Catholic Faith and Order, the Faith and Order which will surely have to be the unreservedly accepted basis of full Christian Reunion.

III. *The Coming Lambeth Conference*

The movements discussed in this chapter will undoubtedly be considered by the Lambeth Conference in 1930, and efforts have already begun to be made to secure approval by that Conference of the proposals involved. That body disclaims legislative power, but the influence of any pronouncements which it may make will necessarily be very great, and may result in subsequent legislative action. It is a large assembly, and reflects in its membership every type of Anglican churchmanship. Therefore, while many of its members are known to be unqualifiedly loyal to the ancient Catholic principles embodied in the Anglican Prayer Book and Canon Law, the fact is certain that other influences make themselves felt in its deliberations; and its utterances have not invariably been free from ambiguities of a nature to encourage dangerous actions and utterances. As I have shown in a previous chapter, the Conference of 1920, in spite of its ecumenical outlook and evident desire not to betray ancient Catholic principles, did give forth ambiguous language. Some of its phrases, in particular, lent themselves to irregularities which have caused disquiet, and have encouraged inferences as to the possibilities of Home Reunion in the near future which can only result in disillusionment. That British Nonconformists are not ready to accept any basis of reunion which would either represent genuine agreement in things deemed essential by Anglicans, or be consistent with Catholic liberties, became quite apparent in the Nonconformist agitation against the revised Prayer Books of 1927 and 1928, and in the parliamentary debates and votes thereon. The state of Nonconformist conviction and feeling towards Catholic principles thereby revealed ought completely to disillusion all Anglicans, official and other, who to any extent accept Catholic principles, as to the practicability of Home Reunion schemes under present conditions.

I do not mean that we should cease to be friendly with Protestant leaders, or refuse to confer with them on our differences. I mean that we should realise that the differences which require removal before reunion between us can either be justified or prove wholesome and permanent are in certain regards vital. We ought, therefore, to confine ourselves to educational action, definitely refraining from schematic proposals. Happily there are Protestant leaders who are friendly enough and broadminded enough to meet us half-way in such non-committal procedure.

My personal views as such can have no perceptible

influence with so august a body as the Lambeth Conference. But I am emboldened to say what I do concerning its business in 1930 by the double circumstance that Protestant-minded advocates are freely seeking to influence the Conference in their direction, and that the principles for which I am pleading are peculiar neither to myself nor to any petty faction. They are rooted in Anglican formularies and the Prayer Book ; and pertain indisputably to the only platform upon which the reunion of Christendom at large is possible. Their surrender or compromise is certain to delay instead of promoting that sacred cause.

It will be a joyful day when the Lambeth Conference gives a clear and unambiguous affirmation of its ecumenical standpoint, and refrains from encouraging hopes and procedures which, in the interest of a Home Reunion unlikely to be achieved in this generation, result in practically substituting provincialism for the ecumenical mind. There are solid reasons for hopefulness ; and, for one, I do not believe that the coming Conference will betray its great trust. May the Holy Spirit guide its deliberations.

POSTSCRIPT

Since completing the body of this book, I have received ' The Primitive Church : Studied with Special Reference to the Origins of the Christian Ministry,' by B. H. Streeter. It approaches the problem of the early development of the ministry from a fresh angle, and is written, as might be expected in view of its authorship, in a scholarly temper and with persuasive skill. I agree with my advisers in thinking that I may well make a few comments on his argument.

Noticing the fact that in the rival theories of the original Christian ministry—Episcopal, Presbyterian and Independent—the common assumption is ' that in the first century there existed a single type of Church Order,' he sets this assumption aside, and bases his enquiry and arguments upon a double hypothesis : (*a*) that in the New Testament itself an evolution in Church Order can be traced ; (*b*) that at the end of the first century there were different systems of Church government in different provinces of the Roman Empire—prototypes respectively of the Episcopalian, the Presbyterian, and the Independent systems. Whether this hypothesis of primitive diversity ' may, or may not, succeed in commending itself to the judgment of scholars,' it has the merit, he thinks, of not being ' likely to add fuel to the flames of ecclesiastical controversy.' He adds, ' Indeed, if my hypothesis is correct, then, in the classic words of " Alice in Wonderland," " everyone has won, and all shall have prizes." ' His method of argument is to make a fresh survey of early Christian literature and to apply his findings *seriatim* to testing his thesis. He thinks he has 'shown' that belief in the existence of one form of Church Order in the primitive Church is 'an illusion,' and that 'Everywhere there was readiness to experiment, and, where circumstances seemed to demand it, to change.' He suggests that 'it may be that the line of advance for the Church to-day is not to imitate the forms, but to recapture the spirit of the Primitive Church.'

For several reasons I do not feel called upon, nor is it necessary for defence of the position taken in this volume, to consider in detail the numerous contentions upon which the validity of Dr. Streeter's general argument depends. Such task will no doubt be undertaken in due course by competent scholars. I limit my comments to certain central and more or less determinative points.

(a) Our author candidly acknowledges that some of the details of his argument are open to dispute ; but he does not seem to realise how numerous, and in some cases how significant, these doubtful details are. They appear in all parts of his volume ; and, as he bears witness, bring him not rarely into opposition to the conclusions of recent experts of the first rank. Granting, as we must, that sometimes his fresh angle of approach justifies his reconsideration of their conclusions, the number of his rejections of them indicates a reliance upon his own speculative opinions which is daring, and is calculated to weaken the convincingness of his general argument for careful readers.

(b) He punctuates the element of 'experiment' in primitive ecclesiastical developments. Such description is plausible but misleading. It implies lack of initial and coherent guidance by the Holy Spirit. What really determined the course of development was a *Spirit-guided opportunism*, the human form of that wisdom with which God waits for suitable occasions in each stage of fulfilling His plans for His Church. The Apostles were His primary agents, and it was their peculiar

L

function to determine under the Spirit's guidance those things upon which the validity of subsequent developments would depend. The principles of unity and continuity were in peculiar need of authoritative safeguarding ; and such safeguarding obviously demanded provision by the Apostles for a continuing ministry and oversight, one of undeniably valid commission from above and authority to exercise pastoral rule in Christ's name. The need of this provision was plainly vital, and could not safely be left to be met by the precarious method of ' trial and error.' This consideration supports the traditional Catholic teaching of many centuries, that the sure guidance of the Spirit controlled the apostolic development, as occasion suggested and permitted, of the threefold ministry of the Mother Church of Jerusalem, and thereby established the norm to be filled up in other Churches whenever circumstances permitted their full and autonomous organisation. The developments in the Mother Church, as being creative, were certainly unique ; but to describe them as ' abnormal ' is surely quite misleading. They *established* the norm.

(*c*) If for argument's sake, and contrary to my conviction, I accept *en bloc* the alleged data with which our author supports his thesis, I fail to perceive the finality of his inference from them. He concludes that the diverse ministerial situations in the primitive Churches show a diversity of ministries analogous to that found between the Episcopal, Presbyterian and Independent or Congregational ministries of our time. The analogy is unreal. The Presbyterian and Congregational ministries have for differentiating marks the performance of ordinations respectively by presbyters and by congregational action. They both presuppose the validity of non-episcopal ordination ; but the lack of *locally settled* Episcopoi (in the final meaning of that title) in the first age does not at all prove the practice of such ordination. No real evidence has been obtained that non-episcopal ordinations, in the later use of terms, were performed, or if performed were accepted as valid, in the primitive Church. The more credible inference to be drawn from the diverse ministerial situations in question is that they represent various stages in the development of missionary Churches, previous to their full autonomous organisation according to the apostolically established norm of the Mother Church. The delay in their being given their own episcopos or episcopoi, in the final meaning of that title, was probably due in large part to cautious missionary policy; and in the meanwhile ordinations were performed, so far as we have evidence, by visitors having what we call 'episcopal' rank. We should not confuse the power of *electing* ministers with that of *ordaining* them. Elections were often of a democratic nature; but ordinations had to follow, and had to be performed by those whom the Church at large would recognise as having received power to ordain. It was thus that continuity of 'mission' and Catholic unity were safeguarded. 'Mission,' derived from Christ through His Apostles, was *de*volved from above, not *e*volved from below.

(*d*) The death of the Apostles, the destruction of Jerusalem, and the disorders emerging in the sub-apostolic period (both doctrinal and governmental), brought acute need for hastening the final organisation of missionary Churches and for emphasising the governmental status of the Episcopoi. And this obviously required the establishment of mon-episcopacy in the several Churches; although, so far as the principle of episcopal ordination was concerned, the apparent transition from collegiate to mon-episcopal rule in certain Churches could make no difference. The promised guidance of the Spirit could not fail in a crisis of such gravity; and we are justified in attributing the imperatives of both Clement of Rome and Ignatius of Antioch to such guidance. They were raised up to lead the Churches through dangers which threatened to bring

destruction to the as yet immature Christendom. Neither
of them resorted to new principles ; but each fell
back upon and emphasised apostolic provisions—
Clement witnessing to the provision for continuance
of overseers, the apostolic succession to which our
author refers, and Ignatius witnessing to the necessity
of the Episcopos, as such we know the Apostles had
appointed in the Mother Church. Dr. Streeter's effort
to discredit the witness of Ignatius as of a neurotic,
dominated by an *idée fixe*, and vibrating between humility
and pride, is inconsistent with his generally fair-minded
procedure. He admits that Ignatius was a genius,
obeying a sense of prophetic vocation. And whatever
signs of overstrain he may think that he discovers in
his letters, he is not justified, in view of the then existing
crisis in the Church, in discounting either his prophetic
consciousness or the congruity of his ' *idée fixe* ' with
what genuine guidance of the Spirit would move such
a leader at such a crisis to urge upon the Churches.

(*e*) I have indicated in this book the faultiness of
method which reduces the value of many modern efforts
to ascertain the truth concerning the origin of the
Church's ministry, especially of the historic Episcopate.
The method referred to sets aside the ancient and broad
stream of tradition concerning the origin of the ministry
and its appointed means of continuance. It is dismissed
in spite of the fact that it emerges in full possession in
an age when immediate listeners to apostolic teachers
were either still surviving or had very recently transmitted their witness. Surely this tradition fixes the
burden of proof upon those who reject its content ;
and this burden is not successfully removed by appeal
to the confessedly fragmentary knowledge of the details
of sub-apostolic developments which these modern
scholars now find it possible to obtain. Dr. Streeter
adopts this mistaken method. He sets a conjectural
reconstruction of only partially verifiable details against
the consentient mind of a Christian age which had

more abundant means of acquaintance with apostolic provisions than he can reasonably hope to secure.

(f) Our author's belief that, if his hypothesis is established, 'Everyone has won, and all shall have prizes' is singularly optimistic; and it reveals no adequate realisation of the principles involved in the controversy which he labours to remove. Two immediate consequences would follow the establishment and general acceptance of his hypothesis. In the first place, it would register triumph of the Independent system, for it would vindicate, theoretically at least, the right of each local Church to choose without interference which type of ministry it would adopt, and to change that choice subsequently if it saw fit to do so. Secondly, it would nullify the Catholic belief, shared in by 'high' Presbyterians but emphatically rejected by Congregationalists, that for permanent stewardship of the mysteries of God an official ministry was instituted by the Lord and His Holy Spirit in apostolic days, with the purpose that it should perpetuate itself in unbroken succession, without substantial change of its original form, unto the end of the world. The major part of Christendom still retains after many centuries the belief that the perpetuation of this stewardship and transmission of the Lord's pastoral commission was devolved under the Spirit's guidance by the Apostles on what subsequent generations have entitled the Episcopate. The authoritative stewardship of divine mysteries is involved, and the reason for insisting upon the Episcopate, and upon common recognition of its divine appointment, is far more than a matter of external government. It is that the Lord's ministerial arrangements for His Church must be perpetuated, if the mysteries which He committed to the Apostles are to be preserved, and are to be ministered without subversive change and without loss of the divinely provided guarantee of valid sacramental functioning. Modern experience proves conclusively that abandonment of the historic Episcopate carries with it the loss of vital elements of the ancient Faith and Order of the undivided Church. I may not omit to remind my readers, in conclusion, that the recovery by non-episcopal Churches of these elements is an unescapable condition of full Christian reunion. Agreement as to the ministry cannot avail for reunion of Christendom, if the mysteries committed to its stewardship are not preserved in their integrity and accepted with sincere general agreement.

Printed in England at THE BALLANTYNE PRESS
SPOTTISWOODE, BALLANTYNE & CO. LTD.
Colchester, London & Eton